Lichtenbergianism

procrastination as a creative strategy

by Dale Lyles

The Lichtenbergian Press

2017

The Lichtenberg Press
an imprint of Boll Weevil Press
bollweevilpress.com

Library of Congress CIP data
Lyles, Dale.
Lichtenbergianism: procrastination as a creative strategy / Dale Lyles.
1. Creative ability. 2. Creative thinking.
153.35 – dc22
ISBN 9780692965962

The author gratefully acknowledges permission to reprint the following materials:

chapter epigraphs: G. C. Lichtenberg's aphorisms, from *The Waste Books*, translated by R. J. Hollingdale (courtesy of Frances and James Hollingdale).

p. 16: "Twin Mystery," by Piet Hein (courtesy of Hugo P. Hein).

p. 61: "Two Sunflowers Move Into the Yellow Room," by Nancy Willard (courtesy of Eric Lindbloom).

ALSO AVAILABLE FROM LICHTENBERGIAN/BOLL WEEVIL PRESS

Agatahi: the Cherokee Trail of Tears, W. Jeff Bishop
Life in the Park: a novel, Marion T. Smith
Another Farewell to the Theatre, Marc Honea
A Cold Coming, W. Jeff Bishop

To VHL, whether she likes it or not

Let him who has two pairs of trousers turn one of them into cash and purchase this book.
— Georg Christoph Lichtenberg, Notebook E.16

Cras melior est.
— The Lichtenbergian Society

Lichtenbergianism

procrastination as a creative strategy

Contents

Foreword

This really should not exist. It doesn't actually matter whether I am referring to the book you hold or the foreword you are currently reading. The same logic applies to both. Foreword and book alike are the product of a group of people that hang their hopes on the dubious notion of putting off until later what you had claimed you would create today. And yet, here we are with a creative work that was (at least eventually) not postponed.

In truth, that is only the first of the improbabilities surrounding the situation. You might also ponder the reality that any insight contained herein all started as a smartass response to an email. I'll not spoil it here, as our author recounts it better than I could, but that is the truth of the matter. In many ways, this book is merely another chapter in what started as a humorous exchange none of us was particularly willing to bring to a proper end.

If you are killing time in the bookstore perusing the dust jacket, or dare one hope, this foreword whilst your significant other shops for something you find incomprehensible, you are probably wondering why a book that should not have happened, that began as a joke, might be worth your time.

Oddly enough, the answer is that the ideas you will find here seem to work.

Wait. What? What do you mean, "work"?

The reality is that what is presented herein does makes a meaningful difference. Our merry misfit band has experienced a transformation since that fateful initial email now so many years ago. We have published, written, composed, acted, led, and transformed careers.

Don't get me wrong. This book does not unlock the dark secrets of creation and success. These things are still hard work, and this road is still only one of many. This is not *THE* way. But it is *A* way.

You may be asking yourself if the topic even pertains to you. Perhaps you don't think of yourself as particularly creative, or maybe your creative endeavors are more of a side-line. If so, then that means you and I (your friendly foreword person) have something in common. While I consider myself creative, others don't typically think of my day job as an overtly creative one.

There have been times in the past when I even questioned if I had credibility within the core group of Lichtenbergians. Their book authoring, play writing, symphony composing, museum curating ways left me with a significant case of Lichtenbergian impostor syndrome. As a guy that wrote software and, later, led other engineers, I found my work schedule left me with less and less time for my passion for acting and the occasional drawing. Had I worked my way out of the club? Had I become an interloper? A poseur? Had the time come to recuse myself?

No and no. First, while my overtly artistic endeavors had certainly been encumbered by my career stage (as opposed to stage career), this invalidates neither their influence nor importance. Further, as the formalism being crafted for Lichtenbergianism continued to take shape, I found more and more unexpected utility for it within my "day job."

I found with increasing frequency that I was recounting to software engineers insights developed in conversations around the fire with my ash-bound brothers.

Sometimes resonance was revealed while providing coaching to those struggling with the switch from a monolithic or big-bang software development approach to an iterative one. The Lichtenbergian notion of ABORTIVE ATTEMPTS is not so different from minimal valuable product and incremental delivery of customer value. Both emphasize getting something on the canvas and both recognize that learnings generated from the imperfect make the eventual product better.

Other times, the overlay was far more personal. When seeking meaning for myself and those around me, I reflected on our many conversations about the creative urge. As in art, engineers are, at root, creators. As with a gifted artist, the work of a gifted engineer will inevitably reflect the artist/engineer. And as also with art, an engineer must eventually ABANDON his or her work and move on.

Ultimately, correlation doesn't equate to causality, and the sample size of our cadre falls well short of statistical significance. Those are all nerd words meant to point out that it is your own experience combined with the resonance you find in these pages that will determine if Lichtenbergianism means something to you. I invite you to consider the ideas you find here. Try them on. Consider taking this unlikely less-travelled road. It has made all the difference to me.

Kevin McInturff: innovator, actor,
engineer, artist,creator

Acknowledgments

Despite my best efforts at TASK AVOIDANCE and ABANDONMENT, it appears that I have written a book.

I must thank my ash-bound Lichtenbergian brothers: Jeff Bishop, recording secretary; Marc Honea, Aphorist; Craig Humphrey; Jobie Johnson; Mike Funt; Kevin McInturff; Michael Jenkins; Daniel Conlan; Terry Maiers; Eli Selzer; Jeff Allen; Philip McInturff; Ted Smith; and Matthew Bailey. Without them, I'm sure I would be puttering around the house procrastinating on some major project. Oh wait…

Thanks to those who read through bits and pieces and gave me their thoughts on the entertainment value of the book as a whole and on the wrong bits in particular. Eli Gaultney has been especially bold and helpful in this regard.

I should probably thank Abigail, Assistive Feline™, for her continuing efforts to support my TASK AVOIDANCE. Cecil, the new Assistant Assistive Feline™, has done his best, but he's still just learning the trade.

There is actually a great deal of philosophical thought behind Lichtenbergianism, but I have no interest in writing a big thick book recapping all the reading I've done. Instead, I've listed in the bibliography the books that have contributed to my thoughts here, and I encourage you to explore them. (In fact, every time you read a book that influences you, check out its bibliography if it has one and follow its lead. After all, TASK AVOIDANCE is more productive than you think.)

Finally, I must also thank my long-suffering Lovely First Wife, who is so averse to the outside world "knowing anything about her" that I will refrain from naming her in this document. Her tolerance of me is what makes me possible.

Dale Lyles: educator, writer, composer,
cocktail craftsman

Introduction

    Before we begin, I'd like to tell you why I think I can write a book telling you how to be creative.

    I am an amateur. I am a dilettante. But boy, am I diligent at it – a diligent dilettante, if you will. Over my long life, I have:

- designed and implemented classroom lessons (I was an educator for 37 years)
- managed a community theatre company for 20+ years, where I directed scores of plays, including straight plays, world premieres, devised theatre pieces, musicals, and Shakespeare; acted; designed costumes, sets, and sound; built costumes and sets; composed incidental music; composed a musical version of *A Christmas Carol*
- directed a church choir
- written poetry
- written a young adult novel
- painted/drawn/sculpted
- designed and landscaped a labyrinth in my backyard and constructed labyrinths for friends
- composed choral/church music; orchestral pieces; opera; song cycles, including a setting of Newbery Award winning *A Visit to William Blake's Inn* by Nancy Willard; chamber music
- written a blog since 2005
- translated *The Marriage of Figaro* and sung the role of the Count

- designed and built websites and databases
- served as an administrator for one of the nation's premiere summer programs for gifted and talented high school kids
- danced, both ballet and historical social dance
- created a theme camp for a regional Burning Man-style event, and ended up designing the site for said event twice
- created some really yummy cocktails[1]

And now I've written this book.

Whether I have done these things well is not the point. The point is that I have *done* these things, mostly because nobody told me not to. The point is that I have spent my life both creating and guiding others through the creative process, and I've learned a few things.

Actually, I've learned a lot of things, and all of them lead to my main idea here: *you can do this too.*

Who's telling you you can't? Let me give you a piece of advice right up front. I call it the Lyles Eternal Truth About Actors, and I give this advice to any uncooperative or fearful actor: "There's no such thing as an actor who can't, only an actor who won't."

So if you want to write a symphony, who's going to stop you? Getting it performed is another thing entirely and is outside the scope of this book, but no one can stop you from writing it.

No one can stop you from writing that novel, or forming a band, or creating a cocktail better than the Quarter Moon.[2] No one can stop you from blogging or taking photographs or painting or landscaping or whatever it is you would love to do but have been too afraid to start.

And the good news is that you don't have to do it today. Or even tomorrow. Procrastination is your friend.

By the way, it's pronounced *lish-ten-BERG-ee-an-ism.*

So that's me. Pleased to meet you.

---

1   The Quarter Moon Cocktail: 1.5 oz bourbon, 1 oz Tuaca, .5 oz Averna Amaro. Stir over ice, strain into old-fashioned glass over ice with orange peel garnish. (You may also do it straight up in a coupe or Nick & Nora glass.) The orange peel is essential.

2   The Smoky Topaz – also by me.

Here's how this book works: the first chapter gives a brief history of Lichtenbergianism and how it grew into this book so that you can see that none of us Lichtenbergians are geniuses. We're just these guys, you know, who like to write and compose and stuff.

The second chapter outlines some basic ideas about creativity and the creative process that are essential to getting the most benefit from the rest of the book. I'll say it here even though I say it again in both of the first two chapters *because it's critically important:* this book will not teach you to be creative. You are already creative.

The next nine chapters each examine one of the Nine Precepts, explaining the basic concept and giving examples. Where possible I have included personal stories from actual Lichtenbergians as well as anecdotes about more famous (and better) creators. I also show how each Precept is linked to the others.

The tl;dr[3] version: *Just do it. Then do it again.* There, I've saved you the trouble of reading the rest of the book.

The last two chapters do a little summing up and a little exhorting to go forth and *just do it*. Eventually .

---

3   That's internet-speak for "too long; didn't read."

Airport Version

I didn't meant to write such a big thick book, I really didn't. I think the Precepts of Lichtenbergianism are easily explained and understood, and yet I've done an awful lot of explaining in the chapters that follow.

If you're standing in an airport bookseller's, wondering if this is the book you want to buy before you hop that flight to Denver, then here's the Airport Version: a one-page description of the Introduction, the Framework, and each Precept in very basic terms. If you never read anything else, you'll have the basic structure of Lichtenbergianism.

Also, this is a great place to take notes on your ideas about the Precepts.

Introduction to Lichtenbergianism

A bunch of guys got together about ten years ago to discuss creativity. They formed the Lichtenbergian Society, named after the 18th-century German physicist Georg Christoph Lichtenberg, who was famous for his procrastination.

Several years later they discovered they were being more productive than ever, even though their motto was *Cras melior est*: Tomorrow is better.

They developed Nine Precepts to explain this paradox.

Framework

All human beings are creative: all humans are born to Make the Thing That Is Not.

That means you, too.

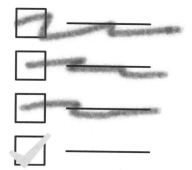

1. Task Avoidance

Cras melior est: Tomorrow is better.

You can be more productive through procrastination by avoiding one project while working on another.

 10w es an ske on, but hey

re awaiting not so much a final

evision as a few more glimpses

f the sun that will make them

2. Waste Books

Always have a way to write down everything.

Come back to it later.

3. Abortive Attempts

Don't wait until you can do something perfectly before you begin.

Write "Abortive Attempts" at the top of your page to let the universe know that it cannot stop you from producing crap.

Produce crap.

Fix it later.

4. Gestalt

GESTALT means "shape" in German.

Once you've started your ABORTIVE ATTEMPT, step back and see what shape it's in. What's missing?

5. Successive Approximation

Once you've assessed your project's Gestalt, tweak the project. Move it closer to being finished.

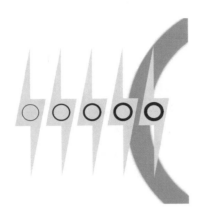

6. Ritual

Have a way to get your brain/soul/ear/eye/hand into working mode.

Create your time and space to create, then protect it.

7. Steal From the Best

Use the past.

Reverse engineer the artists you admire.

8. Audience

You have two AUDIENCES:

1. Those people out there.

2. Those people right here.

(And 3. Yourself.)

9. Abandonment

Three kinds:

1. You can come back to it later.

2. It's ready for an AUDIENCE.

3. Failure is always an option.

Lichtenbergianism

procrastination as a creative strategy

Introduction to Lichtenbergianism

If this is philosophy it is at any rate a philosophy that is not in its right mind.

— GCL, L.23[4]

What is a Lichtenbergian and why does it have an *ism*?

This is not actually a book about procrastination, as useful a strategy as it is.[5] Rather, it is about how a loose-knit group of creative men in a small town upped their game by forming a society the purpose of which was *not* to create anything.

This book will not make you creative – you are already creative, just as every human is creative.[6]

---

4 The aphorisms heading each chapter are taken from *The* WASTE BOOKS, by Georg Christoph Lichtenberg, translated by R. J. Hollingdale. The letter.number tag refers to the notebook where it the original can be found.

5 Instead, see *The Art of Procrastination: A Guide to Effective Dawdling, Lollygagging and Postponing*, by John Perry

6 See Appendix A: The Arts Speech

This book will not free the artistic genius within you. It will not get you a record deal, a Tony Award™, or a one-man show at MOMA.

This book will not give you "creative exercises" to sharpen your skills. There are plenty of other books that are better for that and more specifically attuned to your own area of creativity.

Lichtenbergianism is *not* a prescriptive set of rules or procedures that, if followed, will make you creative. It's not a way to become rich and famous,[7] nor to quit your day job. This is not an instruction book.

This book is not even necessarily for those who make a living through their creativity. However, if you are a Citizen Artist who thinks he/she might like to try writing a novel, or painting a portrait, or designing a labyrinth, but who keeps putting it off for fear of failing – *that* we can help you with.[8]

In late 2007, I sent out an email to a collection of friends noting that the Winter Solstice fell on a Saturday and would anyone like to join me around the fire pit for an evening of drinking, conviviality, and earnest discussion on the nature of art? Since the solstice was the weekend before Christmas, I was surprised when all six men accepted my invitation.

Most of us knew each other through my time at the Newnan Community Theatre Company, where I had been the artistic director for 20+ years. All of us were creative in ways other than theatre – composers, photographers, writers, musicians – and moreover were creative in our careers as well – educators for the most part, but also a reporter, a computer programmer, even a clown.

All of us were at a point in our personal and creative lives where we wanted to sit around a fire and talk about the nature of art with someone similarly inclined. In the intervening weeks, discussion on my blog ebbed and flowed until one day I posted a (very negative) review of the Bavarian State Opera's production of Unsuk Chin's *Alice in Wonderland*.[9]

Discussion in comments became vigorous as we defended/trashed the "old forms" like opera and debated whether they were still viable. Good times.

---

7   from Turff: "Although some of our lot have found it helps."
8   Of course, the professional who finds him or herself in the grip of "writer's block" or frozen perfectionism will find a lot to like in this book too.
9   We were in Munich visiting our son, who was there studying German.

After a particularly vibrant exchange, Turff[10] intoned, "To do just the opposite is also a form of imitation," and credited the aphorism to one Georg Christoph Lichtenberg.[11]

I headed over to Wikipedia to find out who this Lichtenberg chap was and discovered someone after our own hearts: an innovative thinker who puttered around in many fields; a physicist and an educator; an Anglophile, who on a trip to England once visited the widow of the great typographer Baskerville to discuss buying the designer's elegant typefaces.[12]

GEORG CHRISTOPH LICHTENBERG

And then… there was this sentence:

Lichtenberg was prone to procrastination. He failed to launch the first ever hydrogen balloon, and although he always dreamed of writing a novel à la Fielding's *Tom Jones*, he never finished more than a few pages. He died at the age of 56, after a short illness.[13]

"He never finished more than a few pages." Here, surely, was our patron saint. I teasingly assigned everyone the task of writing the first chapter in a "*Tom Jones*-like novel," and we were off. Within a week, The Lichtenbergian Society had a charter, officers, and an agenda for the inaugural meeting.

Our motto: *Cras melior est.* Tomorrow is better.

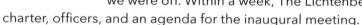

So what does the Lichtenbergian Society actually do? We meet around the fire pit in my back yard, we drink, we talk. We have our Annual Meeting on the weekend before or on the Winter Solstice. We go on Retreat in the fall to a cabin in the mountains. We share and discuss issues online.

That's it.

Then where does this book and its philosophy come from?

10   A Lichtenbergian. There's a complete list of these guys in the Acknowledgments, which you did not read.

11   Lichtenberg is today most highly regarded in Europe for his vast collection of pithy aphorisms, scribbled down in his WASTE BOOKS.

12   Simon Garfield. *Just my type: a book about fonts.* Gotham, 2012. p. 98-100.

13   Georg Christoph Lichtenberg. (2015, June 29). In *Wikipedia, The Free Encyclopedia*. Retrieved 19:35, November 10, 2015, from https://en.wikipedia.org/w/index.php?title=Georg_Christoph_Lichtenberg&oldid=669229256

A very odd thing happened after that first meeting in 2007: despite our claims of being committed to procrastination, every single active member of the Society became incredibly productive. We've produced books, plays, musical pieces, countless blog posts. Careers have blossomed; some have changed completely.

Our annual goals[14] have gotten stronger and stronger, and often we achieve them.

How?

———

It was my privilege to work with the Georgia Governor's Honors Program (GHP) for nearly 30 summers, rising to the position of full-time director of the program, a position I thoroughly enjoyed for the summers of 2011-2013.[15] That final summer, two Lichtenbergians — Turff and Jeff A. — took a week's vacation to come visit. Turff came because he had attended a similar program in Tennessee, and Jeff because he had helped with the theatre audition process for a couple of years. Both wanted to see the program in action.

Since there were already four other Lichtenbergians on campus (myself, Jobie, Michael, and Mike), I posted a Lichtenbergianism seminar on the afternoon activity board for students and whipped up a brief presentation on the history of the group and Georg Christoph Lichtenberg.[16] The rest of the session was simply each of the Precepts in an elegant font on a white background, and the assembled Lichtenbergians talked about how they used that precept in their creative work and in their careers.

The room was, to my surprise, packed with kids, and the presentation went so well that I wish we had videotaped it, if for no other reason than that writing this book would have been a lot easier. After it was over, the non-educator Lichtenbergians expressed amazement that "the kids were taking notes!" Of course they were, I said: 1) that's who GHP kids are; 2) this is very important information and it's the first time they've had it laid out for them. I myself began

---

14   see AUDIENCE.

15   GHP was a four-week (originally six-week) residential program for gifted and talented high school students in all fields. I attended the program as an art major in 1970 and, as we say in GHP-Land, it changed my life forever. The level of intellectual, artistic, and personal empowerment provided by the program can hardly be believed.

16   It actually took place on Lichtenberg's birthday, July 1, 2013.

this process as a student at GHP myself, with my painting teacher Dianne Mize;[17] this is the beginning of that process for these kids.

That's when it occurred to me that our little circle might have something to offer the world. This book comes from that thought.

Lichtenbergianism is a philosophy we take mighty seriously. For a Lichtenbergian, there is nothing more shameful than getting right to work and doing All The Things. It shows a lack of moral fiber, we think, not to be able to avoid one task or another at will. Only slackers like Pablo Picasso, Johann Sebastian Bach, or Anthony Trollope never take a day off.[18]

It sounds completely counterintuitive, but Lichtenbergianism is in some ways like the description of Alcoholics Anonymous in David Foster Wallace's *Infinite Jest*: a rickety structure that shouldn't work, but it does.[19]

Lichtenbergianism is a set of attitudes, of framing, within which it becomes *easier* to produce… something… anything. These attitudes/precepts give *permission* for the creative person to blunder[20] their way through the creative process as a means of achieving personal understanding/satisfaction. And to write that novel. Eventually.

None of the Precepts are new. We are not reinventing the creative process here. Lichtenbergianism is making no claim of originality or exclusivity to any of its components. We are shamelessly STEALING FROM THE BEST.

---

17 http://diannemize.com

18 Picasso created nearly 148,000 pieces of art over his 75-year career. Bach composed cantatas for three years' worth of church services – that is, 209 *surviving* cantatas, and that's ignoring the rest of his output. Trollope wrote for three hours a day, producing 47 big, thick, Dickensian novels; if he finished a novel before the three hours were up, he just pulled out a blank sheet of paper and started the next one. Do you really want to be like these guys?

19 citation needed, but hell if I can find it now. Let's just say it was footnote 90, p.1000.

20 *see Appendix B*: The Invocation

Framework

> The most perfect ape cannot draw an ape; only man can do that; but, likewise, only man regards the ability to do this as a sign of superiority.
>
> GCL, J.115

Before we begin looking at the Nine Precepts, I want to lay out some basic ideas about creativity that are critical to the way Lichtenbergianism works.

1. We are all creative.
2. Creativity is not genius.
3. Beware the impostor syndrome.
4. Make the Thing That Is Not.

We are all creative. Every one of us; it is inborn in us. As I say in my Arts Speech[21], every child on this planet sings, dances, draws, and pretends long before she learns her ABCs or can count to 10. This is true of you, even if you think it's not.[22]

However, most of us don't see ourselves as having the ability to create, because we are cursed to live in an amazing world. We have at our fingertips

---

21   See Appendix A: The Arts Speech
22   Of course you think it's true. You wouldn't be reading this book if you didn't think it was true.

perfect performances of perfect pieces of music, perfect paintings or sculptures, perfect novels, even perfect photographs of perfect gardens – and we have allowed ourselves to believe that this perfection is the natural product of creativity.

It seems clear to us that only creative geniuses can produce such a level of perfection. Mozart is the supreme exemplar of that kind of creative genius, and I think it's important to embrace this truth: mere humans can't do it.[23]

It's important to embrace this: creativity is *not* genius. We all *want* to be creative, and we all *can* create.

So what is creativity, then?

MAKE THE THING THAT IS NOT.
It's that simple.[24]

That's art: where there was not a thing, now there is. A poem, a musical work, a painting, a sketch.

A dance, an algorithm, a solution, a book, a lesson, an exhibit, an article, a movie, a manifesto.

A drumming, a journal, a cocktail, a script, a mosaic, a website, a children's story, a documentary, a photograph.

It's all out there – except it's not, of course. It's out there in the universe, somewhere, but not until we find it and drag it – often kicking and screaming – into our version of reality.

How do we do that? Or rather, more to the purpose of this book, how can we make it possible for us to do that?[25]

Many years ago I encountered a very early version of an e-zine, created in Apple's late, lamented HyperCard. I think it was called "The Bad Penny." Its focus was on publishing work from people anywhere and everywhere, to give

---

23   Professor Peter Schickele reminds us that this is why the completely incompetent P.D.Q. Bach is such a comfort to us: after encountering Mozart, we feel like inadequate parasites; after encountering dear P.D.Q., we feel as if perhaps we could do as well if not better.

24   Ha. As if.

25   Creativity is not limited to artists, of course; I will use the word *artist* to include and connote painters, designers, actors, composers, writers, scientists, programmers, teachers – *et al.*

them an AUDIENCE. In its first issue, the editors wrote a manifesto that contained a key idea that has stuck with me: what the world needs is *more* bad poetry. Create with abandon. Create more and more poetry. Make it happen – flood the world with it. Don't worry whether it's good or not, just write it.

The point was to encourage people to create, and that's the purpose of Lichtenbergianism.

But, you will object, I'm not *really* an artist. I buy those adult coloring books, but I can't *really* create something new. I enjoy my Friday night sessions at the Sip 'n' Paint studio, but I can't *really* paint a *real* painting. I scribble notes in my journal, but I'm not a *real* poet.

Right. So what do *you* call a person who paints or writes poetry or composes a song?[26]

Before we even begin, we must beware of the "impostor syndrome," that still, small voice in the back of our head constantly warning us that sooner or later all the OTHERS will discover that we are not who we are pretending to be. THEY will take a good look at our work, realize that we are a *fraud*, and set up a hue and a cry to alert the others. (Don't you have the image in your head of Donald Sutherland raising the alarm at the end of *The Body-Snatchers*? You do now.) Really, we all feel this way. I feel this way.

I cringe every time I post a new piece of music on my blog or refer to myself as a composer – or when I started posting bits of this book online and pretended to be an author – *because I'm not really*.

Pfft, is my advice to you (and to myself.) There are so many ways to put this: Assume a virtue if you have it not. Fake it till you make it. Just do it.

JUST MAKE THE THING THAT IS NOT.[27]

To recap:

1.   We are all creative.

---

26   Answer key: a painter, a poet, and a composer. If Margaret Keane, Rod McKuen, and Coldplay have earned the title, so have you.

27   We should acknowledge here that for some of us, the Others have not always been imaginary. Author Brené Brown has researched and spoken about shame in our psychological makeup, and she has reported that many people can recall a specific "creativity scar," an incident where they were literally told they had no talent in some field. I myself remember being told in my early teen years that I couldn't sing, and that lasted a very long time. However, since I finished my stint as artistic director at Newnan Community Theatre Company by singing the role of Count Almaviva in *The Marriage of Figaro*, someone was wrong about my abilities. It wasn't me.

2. Creativity is not genius.
3. Beware the impostor syndrome.
4. MAKE THE THING THAT IS NOT.

And what does procrastination have to do with any of the above?

Before we decided to give that seminar at GHP, there really wasn't such a thing as Lichtenbergianism. The Lichtenbergian Society was just us Lichtenbergians doing our Lichtenbergian thing. But as I began mulling over exactly what we would be presenting in the seminar — you know, that pesky *content* thing — my over-organized mind found that within the Lichtenbergian membership certain mindsets and processes seemed to be the rule. So I categorized them into the Nine Precepts of Lichtenbergianism.

1. TASK AVOIDANCE
2. WASTE BOOKS
3. ABORTIVE ATTEMPTS
4. GESTALT
5. SUCCESSIVE APPROXIMATION
6. RITUAL
7. STEAL FROM THE BEST
8. AUDIENCE
9. ABANDONMENT

Each Precept is a loose collection of ideas and principles about the creative process, often overlapping into the others. Lichtenbergianism is incoherent, in the sense that there's no rigor in its conception or application — you can pick and choose and ignore and embrace each part as it suits your needs.

Nor is it linear — you don't "do" the Precepts in order. There is no "leveling up" from Precept Two to Precept Three. They all exist simultaneously in any project you choose to work on, each coming to the forefront of your consciousness as needed.

Lichtenbergianism's value lies in its flexibility and its *permission-giving*: it gives you *permission* to create without the deadly threat of producing something "perfect."

Only Mozart can do that — and he's dead.

Precept 1:
Task Avoidance

The sure conviction that we could if we wanted to is the reason so many good minds are idle.

— GCL, K.27

A parable: He always wears spurs but never rides.

— GCL, J.127

Cras melior est.

— motto of The Lichtenbergian Society

The core value of Lichtenbergianism is procrastination, *not* doing All The Things.[28]

Our society tells us that procrastination is generally supposed to be a bad thing. "Never put off till tomorrow what you can do today" is the sturdy, Puritanical maxim. Clean that house, compose that song, write that chapter, update that website – and do it now! After all, won't you feel better when it's done?

---

28   This is one of those "memes" you've heard tell about. I will be using lots of similar pop culture allusion. I may be old (spoiler alert: I'm old) but I try to stay aware of all internet traditions. [29]
29   That's another meme.

Well, yes, of course you'll feel better when it's done, but first you have to *do it*. Ugh.

To a Lichtenbergian, procrastination is a core principle. Avoiding that symphony, that second draft, that new series of photographs… *That's* a lot more comfortable. *Cras melior est.* Tomorrow is better.

Avoid that task.

But why is TASK AVOIDANCE considered to be a critical Precept of Lichtenbergianism?

Part of the joke is that we think that the world would be better served if artists of all stripes thought twice before releasing their works on an unsuspecting public. It's a matter of quality control, really. It's one thing to crank out the ABORTIVE ATTEMPTS; it's quite another to assemble them and release them as your band's CD. Or book of poetry. Or Southern gothic novel.[30]

We call it the "Better as a T-Shirt Rule," *i.e.*, a witty t-shirt vs. the permanence of a snarky tattoo. Don't commit to permanence when there's still SUCCESSIVE APPROXIMATION to be done. You can always peel a t-shirt off; you can always go back to an unpublished poem and take another look at it. Not so much with a hastily-considered tattoo, nor with a published collection of unrevised diary entries posing as poetry.

It is good when young people are in certain years attacked by the poetic infection, only one must, for Heaven's sake, not neglect to inoculate them against it. — GCL, L.69

Let's face it: 90% of everything is pure dreck. Dreck is fine — see "The Bad Penny" in the previous chapter — because without people having the courage to put their dreck out there, we'd never get the 10% that's actually worth something. God bless all the lesser but nevertheless competent composers that dotted the musical landscape of the Age of Enlightenment, as Professor

---

30   We call these premature releases CORROBORATIVE EVIDENCE and we shake our heads sympathetically – there but for the grace of Apollo – as we consign them to the flames. [*see* AUDIENCE]

Peter Schickele called them — without them, Mozart wouldn't have had a market for his perfection.[31]

But if we, as creators, can hold back our dreck until it's worth at least as much as the bottom 90%, then let's do that. *Cras melior est!*

I want to make it clear that I am not telling you *not* to write bad poetry. On the contrary: you *should* write bad poetry, the more the better. You *should* write execrable death metal music. You *should* make uninspired pottery. That's the whole purpose of Lichtenbergianism: MAKE THE THING THAT IS NOT.

But, I hear you ask, how do we transition from "create a lot of bad dreck, but don't publish it *for the love of humankind*" to "create successful dreck by putting off publishing it"?

Here is the secret to successful TASK AVOIDANCE: because you are an artist, you have more than one TASK to AVOID, each one nagging for your attention. The trick is to play them off against each other, avoiding one by working on another.

This very book (at least at the time of writing this sentence) is being written to avoid the pain of writing music.[32] Not only that, but in the process of writing every section of this book, every other section proved a suitable distraction. Stuck on the AUDIENCE chapter? Jot down that note in your head on GESTALT that has been doing its best to distract you.

The very first full year of the Lichtenbergian Society I failed to achieve a single goal, mainly because I got distracted and built a labyrinth in my back yard instead:

In fact, often the Lichtenbergians find that while we are avoiding our actual creative goals in any given year, we end up achieving something else of value. That's one reason we are offering our quirky philosophy to the world at large: you can actually accomplish more by deliberately doing less.

This is what John Perry calls "structured procrastination" in his charming and perfect *The Art of Procrastination*. I would say that Dr. Perry had beaten me to the draw on the concept, but as I said in Chapter One, none of this is new — Perry

---

31 *The definitive biography of P. D. Q. Bach*, p.23.
32 The opera *Seven Dreams of Falling*. (Still unfinished — I win!)

himself quotes a 1930 Robert Benchley column as defining the concept even earlier: "Anyone can do any amount of work, provided it isn't the work he is *supposed* to be doing at that moment."

As Dr. Perry puts it, "The key idea is that procrastinating does not mean doing absolutely nothing... The procrastinator can be motivated to do difficult, timely, and important tasks... as long as these tasks are a way of not doing something more important."[33]

In 2003, for example, I was given permission by poet Nancy Willard to set her Newbery Award-winning *A Visit to William Blake's Inn* to music. Since there was some interest in performing this piece as part of an international sister city thing, you would think that I would have gotten right down to it. Instead, I spent 2004 writing a children's opera for a competition in Germany — which needless to say I did not win. The good news is that I went on to finish *William Blake's Inn* with an increased confidence in my abilities to orchestrate, and the final result is still my proudest achievement.[34]

The other secret of TASK AVOIDANCE is that *gestation* is a necessary part of the creative process in any model worth the study — and a smart artist uses TASK AVOIDANCE to let ideas form fully. For the Lichtenbergian, it is part of the joke — procrastination is a key to creativity — *Cras melior est* — but make no mistake: we know when we're wasting time and when we're allowing an idea to mature or a problem to percolate unseen.

It is a mistake to think that "creativity" is somehow limited to the actual actions involved in *finishing* a work. Planning — working out the kinks — developing a framework — sketching, doodling, warming up — daydreaming about possibilities[35]_ — these are as responsible for the quality of the finished product as are the actual acts of painting or sculpting or composing or writing.

---

33   *The Art of Procrastination*, p. 3
34   And if you're looking for a world premiere piece for your organization, call me.
35   This is of course distinct from daydreaming about appearing on The Late Show with Stephen Colbert to promote your book.

As Danish mathematician/poet/designer Piet Hein put it in one of his aphoristic poems he called *grooks*:

TWIN MYSTERY
To many people artists seem
    undisciplined and lawless.
Such laziness, with such great gifts
    seems little short of crime.
One mystery is how they make
    the things they make so flawless;
another, what they're doing with
    their energy and time.[36]

It's also true that simply walking away from a project[37] will sometimes allow your subconscious to work in the background on a solution to whatever has been puzzling you. History is replete with examples of great thinkers whose biggest ideas came upon them when they weren't directly thinking about the problem. So absolutely, put down that sonnet and go get in the hot tub. You can thank me for it later.

Another important benefit of Task Avoidance is *slack*. Slack is that extra bit of rope that allows you to make adjustments in whatever it is you're doing with that rope — in Lichtenbergianism, slack is extra time, and it is critical to any adaptive system like creativity.

One of my favorite fables about the importance of slack concerns a secretary in a large firm who was a wonder: she could schedule meetings, make calls, make copies, organize — you name it, she could get it all done for you at the drop of a hat. Then the company hired an efficiency consultant who found that the secretary often had nothing to do, large stretches of time which were not productive. The consultant advised the company to schedule her workload more tightly so that she could get more done.

---

36   Grooks 3, p. 12
37   *see also:* Abandonment

To everyone's astonishment, her usefulness to the company plummeted. She couldn't get to all the things she was asked to do and was often behind. No one could understand it.

They had taken her Slack. All that time she was observed doing nothing was actually her being *available* to take on any task that was asked of her. When her whole day was scheduled, she was no longer able to pivot from one task to another and get them all done.[38]

In Lichtenbergianism, whenever you feel over-structured, rushed, or swamped, it's time for a little TASK AVOIDANCE. Clear out some time for reading, or thinking about another project. Or, if worse comes to worse, clean your house. Ugh.

Just remember that filling every moment with work is not actually being efficient.

There are many ways to manage TASK AVOIDANCE.

You can use some kind of online task management, or an app.

You can do the tried-and-true method of piling all your projects in a pile, or scattered in piles around the house.

You can bullet journal.[39]

You can make a vision board. You could start a Pinterest page.[40]

However, my favorite way of making sure that my TASK AVOIDANCE is productive (and not just laziness) is the Japanese system known as *kanban*.

Kanban was originally developed at Toyota as an inventory control system and has been adapted for use in other areas, such as software design. Jim Benson and Tonianne Demaria Barry have developed a "personal kanban," and I highly recommend their website (personalkanban.com) and their accompanying book.

Kanban involves writing down your tasks and subtasks on cards or sticky notes, then subdividing them into workflow stages such as Ready, Doing, and Done. (Benson/Barry emphasize that the system is ultimately adaptable to your workflow, terminology, and needs.)

---

38 *Slack*, p. 8
39 http://bulletjournal.com
40 Because *that* won't suck up all your time.

The first key concept is called "visualizing your workflow," and the first time you do a kanban dump it's scary: all those sticky notes with all those *things to do*! But take a deep breath and remember: you're going to procrastinate on most of this. You're just getting organized about it.

The second key concept is "limit your work-in-progress." Decide on how many of the sticky notes you're going to actually work on at a time. The usual number is three, certainly no more than five.

As you complete a task, move the sticky note over to the Done column.

That's all there is to it. (Of course there's more to it, but that's it for the basics.)

As Benson/Barry describe the process, the rest of the value of kanban manifests itself through these two key concepts. You start to pay attention to what you're paying attention to. You'll begin to get an idea of the tasks you're avoiding and why. You'll begin to examine your work practices as you watch the flow of sticky notes.[41] You'll begin to adapt the system to your needs.

There are a lot of ways to implement a kanban. The easiest way is simply to take a white board and stick sticky notes on it. (The important thing to remember is that your kanban has to be where you can see it as you work.)

There are of course software versions, including free add-on apps for Google Drive.

For a while, I used my laptop, creating a desktop image and using Apple's Notes app to create sticky notes there.

---

41   see RITUAL

Let's take a look at this for a moment and see how I modified the three-phase model for my own workflow.

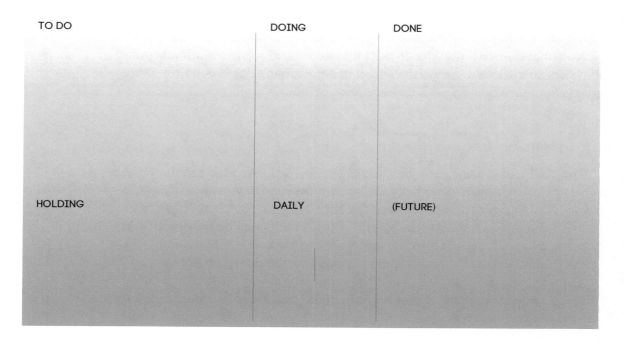

TO DO	DOING	DONE
HOLDING	DAILY	(FUTURE)

Across the top are the three standard columns: To Do, Doing, and Done.

Across the bottom are the modifications I made to the kanban to fit my workflow: Holding, Daily, and Future.

Holding is where I'd put the tasks in the Doing column that I couldn't work on until someone else did their thing, e.g., budget figures or travel plans or something they had to get done before I could move on with the task.

In the Daily section, I put things like *blogging* that I did on a daily basis, stuff that it didn't make sense to keep creating in To Do and then move across the screen every single day. Notice the small vertical line: the Daily section was like a mini-kanban loop inside the Doing column. I could move my *blogging* sticky from one side of the line to the other to check it off – then move it back.

The Future area was stuff I knew I needed or wanted to work on – just not right now.

Your mileage may vary. It *should* vary.

Nowadays I use a system of small cards that sit in a wooden contraption that looks like a small amphitheater. Every once in a while I will look up at it and realize that I really should get busy on one project or another. (Every once in a while I will look up at it and realize that I have either finished a project or ABANDONED it, but hey – that means I get to move a card.)

Note that kanban is not a to-do list. I still have my to-do's on my phone: mow the lawn, do the laundry, prep the labyrinth. My kanban is for MAKING THE THING THAT IS NOT and keeping my TASK AVOIDANCE on track.

———

The Lichtenbergians are not pioneers in TASK AVOIDANCE/structured procrastination. Artists have been doing this forever. Da Vinci was notorious for not finishing work on time or even finishing it at all. It took him fifteen years to finish the "Mona Lisa"; he dragged it along with him as he moved around Italy and even to France. It took him *twenty-five* years to finish "Madonna of the Rocks." Compared to Da Vinci, Lichtenbergians are the Energizer Bunny®.

Giaochino Rossini was just as bad, although he was more lazy than dilatory. The day came for the opening of his opera *La Gazza Ladra* and he still hadn't written an overture, so the producer locked the composer in a room with some burly stagehands. They were given instructions that as Rossini wrote the music, they were to toss the pages out the window to waiting messengers, who would rush them to the copyists. If Rossini didn't write the music, they were to toss *him* out the window.

A brilliant contemporary example of successful structured procrastination is the German artist Anselm Kiefer. Kiefer is known for his often gargantuan paintings that incorporate materials such as dirt, straw, clay, and sheets of lead. They're enormous and enormously beautiful, and they take time for their layers of material to settle in.

Kiefer has several facilities – warehouses, abandoned factories – that he uses as studio space, and he will leave his paintings or sculptures in place for years, even decades, as he works on them. He moves from piece to piece, from studio to studio, rotating his focus and attention from this series of paintings to that body of work. He builds up layers of material as he goes until he is satisfied with the work and declares a painting finished.[42]

Thus, although Kiefer never starts and finishes a painting in what you or I would consider a reasonable amount of time, he's always working and he's always producing. And he does it by *not working* on most of his work.

links & overlaps

How does TASK AVOIDANCE link to the other Precepts? You can put off a project only so long before you're no longer in TASK AVOIDANCE: you've moved into ABANDONMENT. Whether the ABANDONMENT is permanent… well, that becomes a future decision. (You should ask Da Vinci about the difference.)

Remember that the Lichtenbergian mantra *Failure is always an option* is not meant to be a threat to impel you to get to work and MAKE THE THING THAT IS NOT *today*. It's there to remind you that "someday" may never arrive if you don't have a firm grasp of structured procrastination, so it's just as well that you move a project from TASK AVOIDANCE to ABANDONMENT.[43]

TASK AVOIDANCE is also linked to GESTALT through Gestation — a good reason to *not* work on a project is because you're stepping back to see if you can tell what's missing. Some might say that this is actually working — but I say it's a perfectly cromulent example of TASK AVOIDANCE. Any time you're not actively engaged in MAKING THE THING THAT IS NOT, you're safely in TASK AVOIDANCE. No one can blame you — you're not working on it.

Finally, any strategy you use to manage your TASK AVOIDANCE (bullet journals, kanban, scattered piles) should have one major goal in mind: they should leave you with no artistic choice for any given project but to realize that it's time — that project that has hung about, perhaps for years, is now at the top of your list. It's time to move it from the Some Day column to the Doing column. It's time for your first ABORTIVE ATTEMPT.

---

42   You can see him at work in the documentary *Remembering the Future*, http://art.docuwat.ch/videos/art-of-germany/anselm-kiefer

43   It's also permission simply to fail.

and so...

- Practice "structured procrastination" by alternating your projects — avoid working on one project by tinkering with another.
- Kanban[44] your projects — know what you're putting off and why.
- Don't be afraid to let projects simmer.
- Learn the difference between TASK AVOIDANCE and ABANDONMENT.

LICHTENBERGIAN ANECDOTE

At the end of each chapter, I will try share an anecdote written by one of my fellow members of the Lichtenbergian Society, explaining how they have used the Precept in their own creative processes.

However, when I sent out the call for TASK AVOIDANCE, every single Lichtenbergian replied that they were working on something else.

Very funny, these Lichtenbergians.

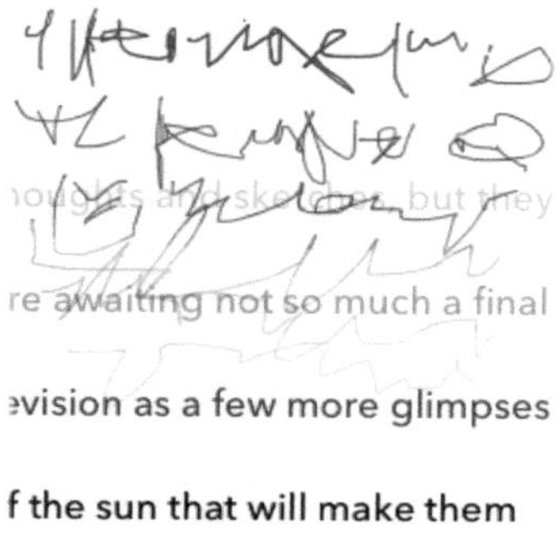

re awaiting not so much a final

vision as a few more glimpses

f the sun that will make them

Precept 2:
Waste Books

Waste-book method highly recommended. A note made of every phrase, every expression. Wealth can also be acquired through saving up truths in pennyworths.

— GCL, F.164

I have jotted down a host of little thoughts and sketches, but they are awaiting not so much a final revision as a few more glimpses of the sun that will make them blossom.

— GCL, B.55

When I first took a deep breath and decided to write this book, I pulled out a little field notebook, slapped a label on it, and started scribbling.

There was no organization, other than the Nine Precepts. It was a brain dump of all the thinking I had been doing about the project: notes randomly jotted down, paragraphs scribbled out of order, each page headed with whichever Precept applied. I poured any and all ideas I had about Lichtenbergianism onto pages without regard to polish or coherence. One idea would spark another; that new idea would become a new page with the appropriate Precept at the top.

Note that I did *not* start by writing the words "Before we begin, I'd like to tell you a bit about me."[45] In fact, the first thing I scribbled was

ABORTIVE ATTEMPTS

2/6/15: J. J. – > Jesu juva

I filled two small notebooks with ideas, sentences, references, questions, and thoughts, until finally, after several months of scribbling, I had the main ideas of this book ready to organize into chapters. I spent a retreat typing my notes into Scrivener[46] and here we are.

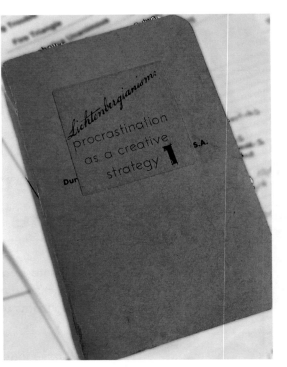

What is a WASTE BOOK? Georg Christoph Lichtenberg got the idea from merchants, who would scribble transactions down in a notebook, willy-nilly as they occurred, then transfer everything neatly to their official account books after the day's business was done.[47] From his student days until his death, he kept a series of notebooks into which he would pour thoughts as they occurred to him: aphorisms, ideas for research, observations, etc.

It's a great idea, one that every creative person needs to consider seriously. *Write it all down* and come back to it later. Stand-up comics especially use WASTE BOOKS, as do poets and other writers, but there's no reason visual artists or scientists (like Lichtenberg) or code monkeys shouldn't do so as well.

Beethoven always carried notebooks around with him, especially as he grew deafer so that other people could write their half of the conversation for him to read, but also to jot down musical motifs as they occurred to him. (We'll revisit Beethoven and his notebooks in a moment.)

The poet Wallace Stevens scribbled down his poetry on envelopes that he kept in his pockets. He did this as he walked to and from his office at the Hartford

---

45   Introduction, p. xiii. In fact, that intro was written *after* I had gotten the book well started – and it is by no means the first version of the intro you read. You did read the intro, right?

46   literatureandlatte.com

47   *The Waste Books*, p. viii.

Accident and Indemnity Company, where he was an insurance lawyer for most of his life — so the fact that you're not a professional creative is *really* irrelevant.

The point is that most artists in the past have used some kind of a system to collect all the bits and pieces that the universe flings at them, and so do Lichtenbergians.

How does it work?

The concept is very easy: just *write it all down*. Key concepts — felicitous phrases — mindmaps — new ideas — changes to old ideas — grocery lists/phone numbers/emails — and then do something with it later.

Here's what is in my current Waste Book (Sep 15–Dec 15):

- restaurants to check out in Flagstaff
- ingredients in good cocktails we had there
- notes on photos taken for blogging purposes
- "tinctured martinis" [a concept that I am still exploring]
- phrases that came to me to express the wonder of the Colorado River
- assorted New Age woo experiences we might be interested in while in Sedona and a possible schedule for fitting it all in
- reminder that someone needed to make the altar for the 3 Old Men labyrinth [my burner theme camp; see below]
- a chart giving the basic grid for my REMS Scale of Woo, and explication of same for blogging purposes[48]
- the name of a chiropractic clinic recommended to me
- a movie recommended to me
- an overview of theme camps/events I was interested in seeing at Alchemy 2015 (one of Georgia's Burning Man-style events)
- questions I had for Newnan Theatre Company before I directed my musical *Christmas Carol* for them
- changes I wanted to make to 3 Old Men processes
- random emails & phone numbers
- Kanban dumps
- notes for this book
- notes for a secret writing project
- design for a travel bar
- notes about my 2015 and 2016 Lichtenbergian goals
- idea for the opening of a brass quintet
- notes from the 2015 Lichtenbergian Annual meeting

48   http://www.dalelyles.com/category/life/rems/

- more recommendations for books/movies
- notes on what I want to fix for the 2016 production of *Christmas Carol*

You can see that some of these are just regular ad hoc things to do, no more than regular grocery lists, as it were. But others are clearly seeds for ideas that I wanted to explore further in more detail in the appropriate context.

It is important to note that WASTE BOOKS are *not* a method to be more productive or efficient. Getting Things Done[49] or Bullet Journals[50] are really wonderful systems, but doing more things faster is simply not in the spirit of Lichtenbergianism. No, as Georg Christoph Lichtenberg says in the second aphorism that heads this chapter, WASTE BOOKS are wild patches of garden where you throw *all* the seeds of ideas without any concern about which ones ever "bloom."

The insanely great choreographer Twyla Tharp uses a similar process, described in her *The Creative Habit*: for every project, she gets a cardboard file box, writes the name of the project on it, and puts into it *everything* that she comes across that will feed the project: recordings, journal entries, newspaper articles, sketches. The box, as she says, "documents the active research on every project."[51]

Most importantly, she says, she uses the box so that she doesn't have to worry about forgetting anything — it will all be in the box, even if it's a project that she's coming back to after sidelining it for a time. Or if she gets stuck on a project, she can rummage through the box and perhaps rediscover ideas and impulses that got left behind during the creation process. All in all, her boxes meet her criteria for a perfect creative system: simple, flexible, functional, and portable.

Sounds like a WASTE BOOK.

As much as I would love to be able to sell you the Official Lichtenbergian Brand WASTE BOOK™ — world domination is my goal, after all — it really doesn't matter what kind of notebook you use. The point is to have something in which you can scribble your ideas without thinking too much about them. Just get it all written into the WASTE BOOK, then later, after the hurly-burly of *your* day, move those ideas your creative space.

---

49   http://gettingthingsdone.com
50   http://bulletjournal.com
51   *The creative habit*, p. 80

These days I'm a big fan of the Field Notes[52] brand notebooks, both their standard notebooks and their spiffy Special Editions. I've also used Moleskine[53] notebooks – who hasn't? – in all their varieties. Lichtenbergian Mike uses plain little bound notebooks, those 3x5 numbers you buy at the dollar store. Daniel, being the youngest Lichtenbergian, uses his phone.

Find your own style for keeping a WASTE BOOK handy. And don't be afraid to have more than one. I keep a general WASTE BOOK in my pocket most of the time, but for each project that I undertake I will have a separate WASTE BOOK: Burning Man; the Backstreet Writers project; *Christmas Carol*; records of letters I've written; each of the plays I've been in; morning pages[54]; major musical works like *SUN TRUE FIRE* or *Seven Dreams of Falling*; this book – each gets a notebook for jotting, journaling, and planning.

Often each notebook gets its own style. For this book, I developed a RITUAL style that helped me get into the frame of mind to work on it: a fountain pen, the WASTE BOOK, and sitting out in my backyard if it were nice weather or inside by a fire if it weren't, with my antique traveling writing desk on my lap. Label each page with the identifying Precept. Bracket any cross-references.

For the Burning Man notebooks, in which I hashed out the philosophical underpinnings to my theme camp (3 Old Men),[55] I used a pencil and wrote everything in all caps.

For *A Christmas Carol*, I planned the reconstruction of a 30-year-old score with charts and graphs, detailing roadblocks and progress.

I even planned my son's wedding ceremony in a special edition Field Notes notebook, plotting out the elements of a RITUAL and writing it out longhand before hand-lettering it in a leather-bound blank book for the day itself.

In our 21st century world, of course, we are not limited to handwriting or paper. I've tried a lot of apps on my phone and computer, but the problem – for me – is that you have to dig through all of them to find one that matches your cognitive/creative style, and even then you're more apt to be learning *its* style than applying yours. I've yet to find one that I have stuck with for more than a couple of months.

---

52   http://fieldnotesbrand.com
53   http://moleskine.com
54   *The artist's way: A spiritual path to higher creativity*
55   At this writing, I have yet to go to Burning Man itself. Regional burns are more accessible, smaller, and cheaper to attend. Alchemy, mentioned above, is one such burn.

The glory of old-fashioned writing-it-down notebooks is that the pencil and the paper adapt to your needs, not the other way around. For example, Field Notes brand notebooks come in four different papers — blank, lined, graph, and dotted grid — but if I want to write in straight lines over the graph/grid, or draw diagrams on a lined page, *I can* — the paper cannot stop me, the pencil must do my bidding.

The first time I added a note to a Burning Man page written on its side — or spiraling around the outside edge — or boxed as an aside — was freeing in all kinds of ways. I didn't have to think or plan linearly[56] — I could let my ideas sprout tendrils and grow in a literally organic way across the pages. I could write down questions when I didn't know the answers, and then answer them on other pages or even other notebooks. (I'm up to four Burning Man notebooks, for example.)

Of course, one advantage of a WASTE BOOK app is that you can dump everything into it and it's always there: you don't have to keep transferring notes or looking back through past volumes to ferret out that note you made on which mountain cabin worked best for your retreat or the book that someone recommended.

If you already have an app that works the way you do, then you should probably keep it. If you want to explore apps because you're more at home with electronics than paper/pencil, then by all means do so. But the moment that you find yourself wishing you could do… whatever it might be that the app won't do… then get yourself a physical WASTE BOOK and see if your thought processes change along with the material format of your recording of them.

Although my discussion of WASTE BOOKS and other Precepts is aimed at you as an individual artist, collaboration is often necessary and desirable in

---

56   *See the King of Hearts fallacy, p. 41*

creative projects, and so I intend to include some examples of collaborative Lichtenbergianism as we go along.

Several years ago, a bunch of us Lichtenbergians were working together (as Lacuna Group)[57] on a performance piece about being a creative person in a small town which largely does not value our creativity. We decided we would work on generating devised theatre bits and pieces — short scenes, interpretive readings, improv — without judgment [ABORTIVE ATTEMPTS] for two years before we tried to make an actual performance of anything.

As we began to work, though, a certain shape began to take hold, and we created the following map:

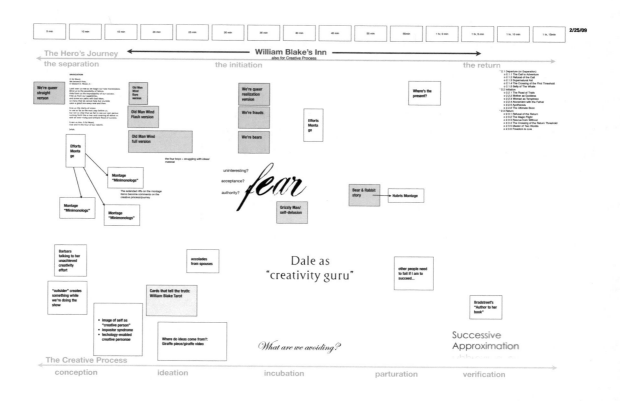

_____

57   an ad hoc theatre collaborative that springs into life whenever one of us needs a theatre collaborative

Perhaps the final performance would look nothing like this, but it would be a good framework in which to place our bits and pieces.

Further, a lot of our work was improvisatory or completely nonlinear and nonlogical, i.e., not scripted and not immediately comprehensible. Many troupes who create their work through improvisation and exploration like this will videotape their sessions so they'll have a record of what they did, but we were not that committed.

However, we didn't want to lose track of cool fragments or impulses, so we started using "image cards":

These were printed on card stock and were available in stacks in the studio. As we worked, anyone who liked a bit could make a note on one of these cards: give it a name, sketch some kind of visual reminder (poses, choreographic notes, gesture drawings) and some kind of verbal description. We would file the cards in the filing cabinet and use them as a resource for future work.

Essentially, we were creating a group WASTE BOOK.[58]

Many theatre groups do this kind of group record thing. Years ago I was in Stratford-upon-Avon and was taking the backstage tour at the Royal Shakespeare Company. We were shown into a rehearsal hall, and I noticed that the walls were covered with photos and printouts. What was curious about them was that they were all about 19th-century England, London in particular. There didn't seem to be anything about Shakespeare anywhere. A year later, *The Life & Adventures of Nicholas Nickleby* opened and became an international sensation.[59]

There are also, of course, online collaborative spaces.

Online collaboration has the advantage of freeing your group from time and space: you don't have to wait until that weekly meeting to share ideas. The

---

58   It goes without saying that we never finished the project.
59   Read all about it in the excellent *The Nicholas Nickleby Story: The Making of the Historic Royal Shakespeare Company Production*, by Leon Rubin.

insomniac can contribute at 3:00 a.m.; the band parent can toss in a note on the bus coming home from the competition.

Many electronic WASTE BOOKS — like EverNote — can be made collaborative, i.e., more than one person can contribute to them online.

One of the simplest online options is Google Docs. It's free, easily available, and easily collaborative: just share your Google Doc file with your collaborators, and everybody can dump ideas there.

You could start a blog: head over to blogspot.com or wordpress.com and you can have one up and running in ten minutes. Make all your co-conspirators editors or contributors and have at it. (Remember that it was a discussion in the comments of my personal blog that started this whole Lichtenbergian business.)

There are more sophisticated options, of course, like BaseCamp, Slack, MindMeister, or Mural, some of which are free and some which are "enterprise" suites, which is code for "costs money." Your mileage will vary with your needs. (Full disclosure: I used Mural back when it was in beta and free; I was very impressed. If I were involved in a major collaborative project again, I'd consider it.)[60]

These online spaces, though, come with costs: it's very easy for ideas to get lost in the shuffle as everyone dumps into a common WASTE BOOK. Google Drive in particular can get very messy if there's not a group librarian managing documents and folders and permissions. But as long as everyone is dedicated and contributing — and has the same general technological literacy! — online collaboration can be useful and productive.

Just remember the purpose: to keep the ideas flowing and recorded!

There are fewer better classic exemplars of the use of WASTE BOOKS than Ludwig van Beethoven. Unlike Mozart, who could write the whole thing in his head and then just transcribe it, Beethoven took a lot longer to work things out, and he did it with a pretty remarkable system.

First, he always carried with him a notebook, a WASTE BOOK, for scribbling in. As he became increasingly deaf, he would give the notebook to acquaintances to write down their side of the conversation, with the result that we have a host

---

60   The internet being what it is, these suggestions may not be around by the time you read this; search "online collaboration tools" to see what's out there now.

of one-sided conversations recorded for us. But he also scribbled down musical ideas that came to him so that he wouldn't forget them. He said that if he didn't write them down, he'd forget them; but if he did write them down, he would never forget them.[61]

If after a while a theme called out to him, he would copy it into a larger, second notebook, where he would play with it, trying out variations, harmonizations, improvisations, until he had an idea of how it would work itself out in a piece. And there he would leave it for a while.

Finally he would open a third notebook and use all his ABORTIVE ATTEMPTS and SUCCESSIVE APPROXIMATIONS to create the new work before copying it all out to manuscript paper.

This was not ever a rapid process: the first appearance of the Ninth Symphony appeared in his sketchbooks a full ten years before the premiere of that work in 1824. His entire life he kept these notebooks with him, even as he moved more than 40 times in 30 years.

links & overlaps

WASTE BOOKS are where many ABORTIVE ATTEMPTS begin. After all, what's the risk in scribbling down an idea that is just the merest mustard seed of an idea? If it never develops, then that's that. The world need never know. If it does, then the WASTE BOOK becomes your friend and tool during the rounds of SUCCESSIVE APPROXIMATION.

The WASTE BOOK process is itself a RITUAL: by establishing a dedicated space for new and undeveloped ideas, for random thoughts, for unexpected revelations, for brilliant inspirations – you've created a RITUAL space. The flow of ideas becomes freer; you know you have a safe space for them, and you know they will be there when you need them.

and so...

- Have a way you can record ideas and plans every day, immediately as they occur to you.
- Have a way to move these ideas into a framework of production.

---

61   Personally, I am constantly surprised to find little things I've forgotten writing in my WASTE BOOKS.

LICHTENBERGIAN ANECDOTE:

MIKE FUNT: PERFORMER AND TEACHING ARTIST

I have kept WASTE BOOKS since before I'd even encountered Lichten-bergianism, and certainly long before I was calling them WASTE BOOKS. As a theatre artist and performer, I was always getting ideas while I was out doing stuff, and in the days pre-smart phone, I was writing these ideas down on napkins, the back of business cards, my hand, a flyer for "How to make $5000 a month working from home!" Anything I could quickly get my hands on. However, these loose leaf missives would often get lost or crumpled or washed after going to the bathroom, and I'd lose the ideas.

So one day I decided I would keep a little notebook with me at all times. I went to the store and got these little 3"x4" composition books. They looked just like regular composition books, only wee. Adorable.

Since then I have carried a notebook with me at all times. I don't always use the mini comp books, but I tend to stick with the cardboard-bound, back pocket/wallet sized theme. Throughout the day I jot down ideas for things I'm working on (*Let's change the line on page 4 to "somewhere other than here."*), things I'd like to be working on (*What if I did a one-man show about the life of Griffith J. Griffith?*), funny signs I see (*Please Don't Take Liberties With Our Animals*), bits of dialogue I hear (*Kindergartener 1: "Why do you always sit next to me?" Kindergartener 2: "I don't know. It's easier than finding someone else to sit next to."*), jokes (*What's the difference between three dicks and a joke? You're mom can't take a joke.*) questions I'd like to look up the answers too (*Why do some pigeons have big white patches? Is that a disease?*), and questions I wonder about, but there probably is no answer to (*Do you think Louis XIV ever had moments where he thought to himself, "You know what? Maybe I'm NOT the human incarnation of the sun."?*). Basically, anything I think might be worth remembering or might serve as inspiration at later date. And, by the way, yes, all the parentheticals are actual notes from my WASTE BOOK.

Once a week I go through all these notes and put them in the place where they are applicable: I fix that line of dialogue in the script; I write a more fleshed out version of the Griffith J. Griffith show, which is now a talk show parody, in my "future projects" notebook; I post that dialogue on Twitter; I google pigeons, I ask every one I know about Louis XIV to no one's amusement; you get the idea. Keeping the WASTE BOOK helps me not to forget the idea. Going through the WASTE BOOK helps to keep it in mind as well as helping to weed out ideas that aren't worth holding onto. Something that was hilarious two drinks into a happy hour might not be as hilarious when I'm rereading it four days later.

However, just because something doesn't get pulled from the WASTE BOOK and categorized that week doesn't mean it gets abandoned entirely (even the happy hour ones). The beauty of keeping all those little WASTE BOOKS is that you always have them to go back to. Then one day when you get accepted into a theatre festival and the theme of the festival is "trees," you can go back to that time you were at happy hour and wrote down just the phrase "clown treehouse," and now you have a jumping off point.

Four years ago I was in a creative slump. I wanted to make a new piece of theatre, but I just didn't know what. I was tapped for ideas, so I went back into my WASTE BOOKS and found one from 2003. In it I found a passage where I had written, "Just read a great story called 'The Day They Hung the Elephant.' I was so moved. I want to do something with this."

"Something," I'd said. I wanted to do "something" with this story. Well, the truth is, at this point I had. I had tried to turn it into a screenplay, which turned out to be mediocre at best, and nobody wanted to hear it. Then I tried to turn it into an animated short, but it just didn't capture the scope of the story, and eventually I abandoned it. In this moment, however, in my urge to create a new show, it hit me like a ton of bricks. "I need to make this story into a play, a clown show." And so I did. After a six months of development and rehearsals, *The Day They Hung the Elephant* premiered to a very well-received production in Los Angeles and eventually a tour around the US. Eleven years after I'd written, "Just read a great story called 'The Day They Hung the Elephant.' I was so moved. I want to do something with this," I did, and it was something I was proud of and that I felt honored the story. But without that WASTE BOOK to refer back to right at the moment I had the drive and the inspiration to "do something" with it, it never would have happened.

As silly as all those little bits of dialogue or quirky signs or random musings seem in the moment, if something is funny or moving or profound to you in a moment, it will be again. Keeping those little repositories of life experience is a necessity as an artist, and will serve as a great tool for you.

Precept 3: Abortive Attempts

Even the mistakes we so frequently make are useful in that in the end they accustom us to believing that everything may be different from what we imagine it to be.

— GCL, J.193

To excuse one's own failings as being only human nature is, provided one has meant well, every writer's first duty to himself.

— GCL, F.74

Don't wait until you can get it right before you start.

In writing this book, I at first was completely stonewalled by my inability to see it in its completed form.[62] This "paralyzed perfectionism" had me creatively stumped. I finally had to make myself start — literally with these words in this WASTE BOOK, this paragraph.

Now I can finish it.

This is a critical concept. Too many times, we think and think and worry about what we hope to have when it's finished — that perfect poem or song or painting

---

62   Full disclosure: now that I *am* writing it, I still can't see it in its completed form.

– and so we never start because we can't see how we're going to make it that perfect.[63]

This is a huge mistake. Just start. It will be wrong, and that's okay. Let me show you why.

Whenever he sat down to compose a new piece, Johann Sebastian Bach would first write at the top of the page, *J.J.*, i.e., *Jesu Juva*, which translates as "Jesus, help!"[64]

A waggish modern translator might say, "Help me Jesus!" – but for J.S. Bach, it was a matter of faith that without some kind of divine intervention, the piece he was about to write would never get off the ground.

Bach: the master improviser, sure-footed at court or chapel, endless source of endless, glorious music – did he really fear starting a new work? Did it not all flow straight from his head to his pen to the paper in eternal perfection?

It may seem as if it largely did, as it did with Mozart and, as far as we can tell, Shakespeare. Apparently, though, even Bach had no idea what he was going to end up with. He just begged God for help and started.

He is not alone. Nearly every artist who speaks about his or her process will say the same thing: "The hardest part of writing/composing/painting is getting started, so I just go ahead and create crap that I can throw away if I need to." Anne Lamott calls it her "shitty first drafts."[65] Nancy Willard called it "Wasted Efforts." The Lichtenbergians call it ABORTIVE ATTEMPTS.

The whole point of writing ABORTIVE ATTEMPTS or Bach's *J.J.* or Willard's *wasted efforts* at the top of your page is to give yourself permission to fail.[66] You disarm the Critic in your head by telling him ahead of time – "this piece, this drawing, this poem, is going to be *crap*. I am *deliberately* going to put down whatever comes into my head or my fingers and *there's nothing you can do to stop me.*"

The Critic doesn't believe you, of course; he knows what you're up to, and he waits for the moment when you stop merely putting crap on the page and

---

63   Spoiler alert: it will rarely, if ever, be that perfect. So you might as well start.
64   When he finished, he wrote *Soli Deo gloria*: To God alone be the glory.
65   *Little Bets*, p. 53
66   see *Appendix B*: The Invocation

instead start trying to make it "good." Then he's ready to swoop in and tell you that it's not good.

So don't try to make it "good." Just keep moving forward, adding new bits and pieces, loops, backtracks. Scratch stuff out. Paint stuff over. Take stuff apart. You'll know when it's time to make it "good," and it's better if you don't try to force the issue until that time, because if you do, you'll simply find yourself at another dead end.

Every musical work I create begins with a Finale® file that I name "[piece]_ ABORTIVE ATTEMPTS." I'll throw some notes on the screen, trying to solve the problem of melodic line, or harmonic progression, or setting of a lyric. It may be only two or three measures long — it almost always sucks — and that's the point. It's going to suck and there's nothing you can do about it.

Not true — there *is* something you can do about it: you can skip a couple of blank measures, drop in a double bar, and plop out another piece of crap. Repeat as necessary. Sooner or later you will hit upon something that appeals to you. (Truthfully, I will often grind out about ten different versions of a theme only to discover that the one that works best is the first or second one. The struggle is real.)

Do not get the false impression, however, that once you've plopped out all the ABORTIVE ATTEMPTS and you've started polishing all those plops into something lovely, you will not hit another dead end. Because you will. The creative process is nothing but dead ends.

"[I] just keep squirting out little turds of creativity — eventually it should be a pile of shit so big that it has to have a pony in there somewhere, right?"[1]
— From a letter to Mike Funt, 2/16/2015

---

1   The joke goes, "A couple had a son who was so optimistic and Cheerful that they feared for his safety in life. A psychologist recommended that instead of giving him toys for Christmas, they give him something disgusting like a pile of manure. So on Christmas morning, he tiptoes down to the living room and sees the huge pile of dung — whereupon he squeals with delight, runs to get a shovel, and starts digging. Flabbergasted at his son's relentless positivity, the father asks, "What are you doing? You just got a big pile of manure for Christmas — aren't you disappointed?" The son replies, "Are you kidding? Look at how big it is — there's got to be a pony in there, right?"

I once set myself a goal of nothing but dead ends called the 24 Hour Project. I asked people to send me three numbers, each of which had a specific range (1-5, 1-540, etc.) Those led me to a specific line on a specific page in one of five books of poetry, so essentially my friends were randomly generating my source material. I would copy the line onto a sticky note and line it up on my monitor.

Then I would announce via the blog that I was starting the next one, and I had 24 hours (defined as midnight of the following day, so I cheated) to set it to music, for baritone voice and either piano or string quartet.

The point was that I prevented myself from making any of it "good": I had to create a tiny little piece of a piece on that one line. It didn't have to have an intro, nor did it have to make sense within any larger context, nor did it even have to be good. It just had to exist by the midnight of the next day.

I did this for six months and generated quite a few 24 Hour pieces, some of which were facile, some were awful, and a few went on to become full-fledged pieces. The project was extremely helpful for me in several ways. It broke me of trying always to create something perfect, and it gave me experience in creating a *lot* of material from which I could draw inspiration later.

So if much of what we do as we MAKE THE THING THAT IS NOT is not going to succeed, then it seems obvious that we should "fail quickly to learn fast."[67]

The summer I took over as director of the Georgia Governor's Honors Program [GHP] is also the summer the program was cut from six weeks to four because of budget issues. What had been possible in the arc of a six-week program — in theatre, dance, music, art, science, agscience, all the areas — was no longer possible. Since successful completion of tasks/projects was mostly out of the question, we focused even more strongly on process, specifically the inevitability and desirability of failure. "Fail quickly to learn fast" became our mantra.

The following January, my local school system invited me to their breakfast honoring that year's crop of nominees. Afterwards, I met with some of those nominees along with three of the previous summer's participants. I talked about the willingness to fail as an important trait to exhibit during the upcoming interview process, and the three alumni laughed and shared — proudly — their failures from the summer before.

One of the nominees asked (rather snidely, I thought, considering she was sitting next to the director of the program), "So what happens if you don't fail?" In one of the proudest moments of my career, one of the alumni responded brightly, "Then you're doing it wrong!"[68]

---

67   *Little Bets*, p. 53 et seq.
68   Nathan, I'm pretty sure you were just being snarky, because gifted. But you were right.

This willingness to go beyond safe boundaries and risk failure in order to gain new knowledge and skills is at the heart of creativity, either in the arts or the sciences.

Several years ago, some of my Lichtenbergian buddies decided it had been too long since we had done theatre and conceived a desire to perform Shakespeare's *Coriolanus*, of all things.

But none of us wanted to devote the time it takes to stage a show — especially Shakespeare — all the weeks of rehearsal, building sets and costumes, setting lights — we just wanted to work on Shakespeare. Plus, we had no theatre space, because we were not a "theatre."

We decided therefore to take an extremely minimalist approach. We would meet only twice a week, Wednesday nights and Saturday mornings, which is when the dance studio was available. There were seven of us, all men, and we would play all the roles in this sprawling tragedy. We would not cast the show before we began working, and, most crucially, no one would direct. We would collaborate.

What followed was a fascinating process: every session was nothing but ABORTIVE ATTEMPTS — we polished nothing, we dropped in and out of scenes willy-nilly, we claimed roles and relinquished them, we cast each other and were ourselves cast in nearly random order.

We would discuss what scenes were "about." We suggested alternative interpretations of theme, plot, character. If anyone questioned a characterization or an artistic choice, then we'd do the scene again to test the objection. We included more than we threw out, and we threw out plenty.

Finally, after we had worked our way through every scene in the play, although not in order, we realized we had about a month before the date we had set for our performances in a public park. We had to stop "playing" and nail some things down — first and foremost who would be playing which roles. We filled the leads, looked at doubling possibilities, and began to rehearse the play in earnest.

Because of what we had learned in eight weeks — sixteen sessions — through our ABORTIVE ATTEMPTS, we were able to assemble the show in the three weeks remaining to us, and on a couple of days in mid-October, seven men in green khaki cargo pants and black t-shirts held an AUDIENCE on blankets and lawn chairs rapt with the politics of ancient Rome.

This experience with *Coriolanus* taught me a lot about risk-taking: it's almost *always* okay to fail as you're starting a creative project. In fact, it's okay to fail all the way from ABORTIVE ATTEMPTS through SUCCESSIVE APPROXIMATION to the very end when you ABANDON your work to an AUDIENCE. Looking back now the casting of *Coriolanus* – the blocking – characterizations – looked *inevitable*, as if some theatre genius had taken the reins from the very beginning and told us exactly what to do – and it's very hard to believe that it was all a series of failures even though I was there when it happened.

Here's a pro tip: all those false starts and dead ends are not trash. Don't throw them away; they're still perfectly good. I myself have on occasion suddenly discovered a use for a 30-year-old melody that I've just kept floating around.

Writers of popular music back in the day had what they called (and are still called) "trunk songs." They'd churn out a number for a show or a star, but it was rejected for whatever reason during rehearsals. They'd put it in the trunk with all their other rejected songs. Next show or album, when they needed a jazzy, slow ballad or a jaunty schottische, the composer had a trunk full of songs that might just fit the bill.

In fact, some of Rodgers & Hammerstein's biggest hits were trunk songs. They were not written for the show they now live in – and unless you go and read up on the history, you will never know which ones they are.

In the 1950 movie *Three Little Words*, the career of songwriters Bert Kalmar and Harry Ruby was told through their songs, and one of the running gags was Harry Ruby's repeated attempts to get his partner to use this snippet of melody that kept bugging him. No matter the assignment, Ruby would start playing that phrase, trying to fit the lyrics to it – and it never worked until (of course) the finale of the film, when the lyric "Three Little Words" just fell into place and became a hit song.[69]

---

69   That plotline, like much of the movie, was fictive.

Here's another pro tip: One of the biggest mistakes an artist makes is what we call the King of Hearts[70] Fallacy: "Begin at the beginning, and go on until you come to the end: then stop."

We have this image that an artist sits down to write her novel or compose his sonata or write their poem — and she just launches right into it and works straight through until she's through. Then she writes The End and we all live happily ever after.

Oh, he might have to stop every now and then because he doesn't know what comes next, or she gets some kind of romantic writer's block, or they have to rethink the main theme — but that's just a hiatus in the long course from start to finish. Soon whatever blockage he's invented for himself is gone, and he picks up where he left off and it's tutti all the way. The End, roll credits.

This vision of how an artist creates a work from start to finish is a myth. No one (but Mozart) can do that, and it is counterproductive to try.

It's OK not to have the entire project planned or envisualized before you begin. For every J.K. Rowling with her seven shoeboxes of index cards, there are more than a few J.R.R. Tolkiens who have no idea where they're headed when they start.

Tolkien started *The Lord of the Rings* as a sequel to *The Hobbit*, i.e., another children's book. Bilbo was named Bingo; Strider was a Hobbit ranger; Sauron was nowhere in the picture. As Tolkien says in his Foreword to the Second Edition to *The Lord of the Rings*,[71] "The tale grew in the telling." Those who believe that artists work straight through from beginning to end are well advised to read all eleven-million volumes of Christopher Tolkien's study of his father's work, *The History of Middle-Earth*.[72]

Even Rowling, who famously planned all seven Harry Potter books before she began to write the first one, found herself tripped up by a plot detail in *Goblet of Fire*, necessitating a hurried rewrite that resulted in the infamous error in the final showdown between Harry and He-Who-Must-Not-Be-Named.[73]

And so when it's time to write that essay or poem or to compose that song, *you don't have to start at the beginning.* Start with the part you know. That may be the conclusion or the climax or the chorus or the hook or whatever has

---

70   *Alice's Adventures in Wonder-Land*, Lewis Carroll
71   *The lord of the rings*, p. xxii
72   Tolkien, C. (2001). *The complete history of Middle-Earth*. London: HarperCollins. This is all TWELVE volumes of The History.
73   Why yes, I do have both the original edition and the corrected edition (American *and* British). Why do you ask?

popped into your head. Just get it out of your head and into reality. From there, it's a matter of SUCCESSIVE APPROXIMATION.

Or maybe you're a planner, someone who maps it all out before beginning. That's okay, too, but be very wary of that map becoming a roadblock. Treat everything as an Abortive Attempt, even your most meticulously planned project. There's a great passage in John Fowles' *The French Lieutenant's Woman* where the narrator is following his character Sarah Woodruff back down the path to the village when she suddenly veers from the path. Astonished, he comments on what he had planned for her to do versus what she decided to do on her own, a great metafictive moment that describes how our art can — and *should* — sometimes take control of what our feeble human brains think is the goal.

> I couldn't wait for success, so I went ahead without it.
> — Jonathan Winters

links & overlaps

ABORTIVE ATTEMPTS, of course, are only the beginning. It is almost always a mistake to believe that the first thing out of your brain is ready for an AUDIENCE. Mortals just don't work that way. Unless you're Mozart or Bach or Shakespeare, you're going to have to test that ABORTIVE ATTEMPT against an AUDIENCE — or if that's too far, against your own sense of GESTALT. Chances are, what you discover is going to lead you back into SUCCESSIVE APPROXIMATION.

and so...

- Give yourself permission to fail by labeling each page with ABORTIVE ATTEMPTS.
- Deliberately set out to create crap — lots of crap.
- Plan if you must, but be aware that art has ideas of its own.
- You don't have to begin at the beginning.
- You can always go back and fix it. [SUCCESSIVE APPROXIMATION]

LICHTENBERGIAN ANECDOTE

Jeff Bishop: author, playwright, public historian

Back in the late 1990s, I thought I wanted to be a screenwriter. In those days, before YouTube and iPhones, the only way to get your works into the production pipeline (without existing IP) was to write spec scripts and hope they made their way out of the slush pile. Mine remained slush. So rather than waste my time on yet another project that had almost zero prospects of ever gaining an Audience, I decided I would scale back my ambitions and write something for the tiny community theatre back in my home town. (A small Audience was better than no Audience.) I was friends with the artistic director, after all. Surely he could squeeze me into the black box during summer season, right?

I had become enamored with Native American history and myths, so I thought I might do something on the very early history of our region. I immersed myself in James Mooney's massive ethnographic works, the biographies of early Scottish traders among the Creek Indians, and expensive, long out-of-print tomes on the lives of early settlers like J.P. Brown's Old Frontiers.

I had intended to spend maybe six months on research, but as it turned out, it was a rabbit hole I wouldn't pull myself out of for over a decade. The research end of it eventually led me into several paying gigs for the National Park Service, documenting Cherokee places like the Chief John Ross House and the Running Waters council ground.

I tried to write the play I had originally envisioned a number of times, but each was a false start. Nothing I tried felt authentic. I scrapped a number of versions before finally completing what I called *Sun Gone Down*, a kind of musical approach to the tale of the struggles between early white settlers and Cherokee leaders like Dragging Canoe and Old Tassel. I felt good enough about it to share it with the folks at the theatre back home, but they showed little interest. I also shared the play with friends I had made in the Cherokee Nation, but they never responded.

So was that decade's worth of research all for nothing? Hardly. Besides turning all of that study into a new history degree, a thesis, and a full-length non-fiction book, I also took the basic musical ideas (and even some entire songs) from *Sun Gone Down* and cannibalized them for a later play – *Flies at the Well*, a much superior play[74] – that brought in massive hometown crowds and a hefty profit for the theatre company.

---

74   available at bollweevilpress.com

Over the course of ten years, my ABORTIVE ATTEMPTS, though devastating at the time, ultimately led to success. And the best may be yet to come (in the form of a still-gestating mythic poem, no less). It's a cliché, sure, but my Lichtenbergian experiences taught me you must first fail – perhaps many times – before you can succeed.

Precept 4: Gestalt

A good method of discovery is to imagine certain members of a system removed and then see how what is left would behave: for example, where would we be if iron were absent from the world: this is an old example.

—GCL, J.258

Back when I was a wee middle school person, I was involved with the local community theatre, The Newnan Playmakers. The group had a pretty illustrious past – their production of Shaw's *Pygmalion* was the first play I ever saw and is the reason I became a theatre practitioner in the first place – but as all groups do, they were experiencing a downward trend. By the time I became their sound guy (and general walk-on), they were reduced to more typical community theatre scripts.[75]

One of the directors of the group was the late Herb Bridges, owner of the world's largest *Gone with the Wind* memorabilia collection and author of several books about the movie. To this day, the only note I can ever remember his giving a cast after a rehearsal (which typically was just a run-through of whatever scenes we were working on) was, "Well, it's good, but it needs work."

---

75   Which also influenced me – when I got to be in charge we didn't do that crap.

Not that he ever actually intervened to make it good: Herb, like all of us at the time, had no actual theatre training, just a love for performing, and I say, God bless him. (God bless us every one!) His little shibboleth became a byword, though. "It's good, but it needs work," we would chorus long after Herb left the group to focus on his collecting.

We were mocking (most unkindly) Herb's lack of ability to tell us exactly what needed work, but at least he had the concept of GESTALT down.

———

GESTALT[76] is German for *shape*, and it has come to mean in English "the shape or sense of the whole," *i.e.*, everything that lies within or belongs to a concept or image, its totality. In Lichtenbergianism, GESTALT is the stepping back from your work and viewing it as if it were finished – complete – because if it *is*, then Calloo! Callay! – you're done.

But it's not – it never is[77] – so what you're doing by looking at your work as if it were complete is trying to see the GESTALT of the thing – the *shape* – of what it *should* look like, *would* look like if it were complete.

Take a look at your work, squint at it sideways, and try to see what's wrong with it… Can you describe what's wrong? Are you able to see/hear it? A touch of blue in the lower right-hand corner? The fourth line of the sonnet sounds clunky? The musical phrase sounds repetitive – or not repetitive enough? Is it too short? Too long?

In other words – what's missing?

That's GESTALT.

You might think that GESTALT means stepping back, seeing *exactly* what's wrong with your piece, stepping back in, and fixing it. And then you're done.

Alas: there is not, somewhere out there in the Empyrean, a Platonic Ideal of your work, a predestined perfection that you will end up with if only you're clever enough to see it. No, the universe is infinite, random, and infinitely random.[78] There is no *one* "right way" to finish your work – there are a great many finished products that can be made from your unfinished block of stone.

Author Scott Berkun describes this part of the creative process in his book, *The Dance of the Possible*. He, too, explodes the idea that you start with your

---

76 pronounced geh-SHTAHLT
77 see ABANDONMENT
78 And randomly infinite.

idea and then proceed smoothly to the finished product. This never happens, he says, unless you're making macaroni and cheese for the 500th time.[79]

Instead, he points out that every choice you make on a project opens up a number of new choices, and those choices open up other new choices, so that rather than narrowing in on your perfect project your creative choices threaten to grow exponentially beyond your control.

GESTALT can be viewed, then, as a strategy for optimizing your choices as you MAKE THE THING THAT IS NOT. When you pick Option A as your best option, then all those choices that sprang from Option B or C can (probably) be disregarded.

Eventually, after what seems like an infinity of new available choices, you'll find that the number of choices you have to make become narrower and narrower until finally you can choose to call the painting/song/cocktail finished.

Here's an extremely meta example of GESTALT in action: since beginning to work on this book, I have restructured the order of the Precepts twice.

Here's the original order (with the current numbering):

1. TASK AVOIDANCE
3. ABORTIVE ATTEMPTS
5. SUCCESSIVE APPROXIMATION
2. *WASTE BOOKS*
6. RITUAL
4. *GESTALT*
7. STEAL FROM THE BEST
8. AUDIENCE
9. ABANDONMENT

As I began explaining the Precepts in actual settings with writers, I realized that although they are not linear they would make more sense to newbies if WASTE BOOKS came second (especially since I was handing people a WASTE BOOK and telling them to use it right off the bat), and if GESTALT were moved closer to ABORTIVE ATTEMPTS and SUCCESSIVE APPROXIMATION as part of the nitty-gritty of MAKING THE THING THAT IS NOT.

---

79   *Dance of the Possible*, p. 69.

And so I reordered them:

1. TASK AVOIDANCE
2. *WASTE BOOKS*
3. ABORTIVE ATTEMPTS
5. SUCCESSIVE APPROXIMATION
4. *GESTALT*
6. RITUAL
7. STEAL FROM THE BEST
8. AUDIENCE
9. ABANDONMENT

Then, as I worked further with people to understand their own processes and how Lichtenbergianism could be helpful in their thinking, it became clear that GESTALT should come *between* ABORTIVE ATTEMPTS and SUCCESSIVE APPROXIMATION. After all, before you can dive back in and successively approximate, you have to step back to see what it is you need to do.

So I reordered them again:

1. TASK AVOIDANCE
2. WASTE BOOKS
3. ABORTIVE ATTEMPTS
4. *GESTALT*
5. SUCCESSIVE APPROXIMATION
6. RITUAL
7. STEAL FROM THE BEST
8. AUDIENCE
9. ABANDONMENT

Because I allowed myself to be alert to the GESTALT of the Precepts, what had been an almost random list of key concepts became an almost coherent philosophical system. I had to reorder the chapters in the Scrivener file – which means I had to drag and drop some things – but otherwise the universe was not disturbed. Well, other than my having to redesign the t-shirts and mugs at the Lichtenbergian CafePress store.[80]

One concept embedded in GESTALT is that of boundaries: knowing where the fences are — and then going beyond them.

The poet Wallace Stevens often used the image of a walled garden to illustrate the nature of creation. Our universe is wildly random, a jungle of input. Every human organizes as much of that wilderness as he can and makes a garden of it — walled off from the chaos beyond.

A *creative* human looks for a door in the wall: a way out, a way beyond, a way into the chaos to bring more of it into line with her vision. Less chaos, more garden.

But how scary is that? Beyond the safety of our garden there be dragons. There's darkness. There are no paths but those which we make. What if we can't find a path or make a path? What if we return to our garden defeated, empty-handed?

It happens. Sometimes the Hero's Journey ends in ashes.[81] But the chaos is always there for us to strike out into whenever we can get up the nerve.

Just remember: If you find yourself out there and can't quite seem to get any of the jungle organized, that's OK. It's an ABORTIVE ATTEMPT. Come back later. Try again.

Wabi-Sabi is a Japanese aesthetic term that enshrines imperfection as a requisite for beauty — "imperfect, impermanent, and incomplete."[82]

One summer I was making a video on behalf of GHP, trying to define for all those nominating teachers back home the kind of kid we were looking for. I was in the art building and was fortunate enough to stumble on the following scene:

---

80   You should have ordered them early; the wrong ones are collectors items now, just like the original edition of *The Goblet of Fire*.

81   see Appendix C: The Hero's Journey

82   *Wabi-Sabi*, p. 7

Andy[83], the intrepid ceramics teacher, was breaking the news to a young artist that her piece had shattered in the kiln. This piece was a female torso, part of an assemblage the student was planning, and the first of its kind – clay, modeling, sculpting – that the student had ever done.

And here was Andy telling her that her boobs had blown up.

Her meltdown was perfectly charming: an even-keeled kid that maintained her sunny composure most of the time was simultaneously despairing at the destruction of her piece and extremely amused at the image of her boobs exploding in the kiln. (There were air pockets, apparently.)

Even worse, a fellow artist who wandered into camera range for emotional support was told that when her boobs exploded, they crushed his "little man." The hilarity was general.

Soon, though, the grim reality took over and she began to keen that her piece was ruined.

"Naw!" roared Andy. "We can fix this. It's going to be OK. We can fix this."

She looked doubtful but allowed herself to be led back down to the ceramics studio where she would begin, literally, to pick up the pieces.

I caught up with her a day later. She was sitting before her "ruined" torso, its breasts just ragged circles where the clay had self-destructed. She was happily daubing an oxide glaze onto it, chatting about how once Andy had gotten her to look at the piece *as it was* and not *as it was supposed to be*, she began to see the beauty in its imperfections and was now disposed to see the catastrophe as an improvement.[84]

Andy did the same for me a couple of summers later when I went to make a bowl for the center of my new labyrinth. The bowl was coil construction, thick and heavy, and Andy must have seen the future even as he coached me through the building of it.

Of course clay that thick will not dry evenly no matter how you stack it, and so the bottom of my bowl soon developed cracks that seemed irremediable.

"Not a problem!" roared Andy.[85] "We'll just fill those in with more clay!" Which we did, but to no avail: the cracks returned and widened. I may have repeated my vain attempts, but in the end the piece went into the kiln and came out with a perilous network of cracks across its bottom.

---

83   His real name. No point in changing anything to protect him. Well, not in this story, anyway.

84   The piece was in fact selected for the juried final exhibit. It completely worked.

85   Andy always roars.

"Not a problem!" roared Andy. All I had to do was buy this particular kind of marine putty when I got the bowl home and patch the cracks with that.

I did, and here was this big, lovely bowl with a bottom of hieroglyphs scrawled all over it. I decided, in the best Japanese tradition, to gold-leaf the puttied cracks.

And now I have this mystic bowl as the center of my labyrinth, and in my meditations various out there, the arcane circles and arcs writ in gold have often played a major role.

Every step of your process opens up new choices, and if a choice results in unexpected outcomes, you may be tempted to chuck it all and sit in the ashes and all alone beweep your outcast state. It may be that your work is ruined and you need to toss it in the trash, but mostly that is not the case. The point is, accidents happen, and they may not be the disaster you thought they'd be: like the young art student, look at your work *as it is*, not as it is *"supposed" to be.*

Pay attention to your accidents. During orchestration of Icarus's aria in the first scene of *Seven Dreams of Falling*, for example, I was working on a climactic moment, and I copy/pasted a line from the piano score into the wrong measure in the orchestral score. I didn't realize it until I played back the section I was working on, but I heard my mistake immediately: the phrase was out of sync with its surroundings.

And it was better.

That didn't necessarily make me feel better about my skills as a composer, but you better believe I took it.

In his *Finishing the Hat*, Stephen Sondheim talks us through the creation of his musicals up through 1981, bit by bit, song by song. In the chapter on *A Funny Thing Happened on the Way to the Forum*, he describes one of the clearest examples of GESTALT that I've ever heard.

First of all, understand that *Forum* is one of the three funniest plays in the English language. (Those would be *Forum*, *The Importance of Being Earnest*, and whatever you choose to be the third.) So it is hard to believe that it was met with "scathing reviews from the critics and indifference from the AUDIENCES" during out-of-town tryouts in New Haven. Director George Abbott was baffled, and he was one of the theatre world's most famous "play doctors," i.e., someone who could walk into a room and tell you immediately why your show was not working.

"I guess we'll have to call in George Abbott," he quipped. Instead, they called in Jerome Robbins, another theatre legend. He watched the show and pinpointed the problem: the opening number.

It was called "Love Is in the Air," and it was a sweet, upbeat number informing AUDIENCES that the play they were about to see would involve hopeless romantics. As Robbins put it, it was "breezy and charming and welcoming and the AUDIENCE enjoyed it, and it killed everything that followed." The AUDIENCE was led to believe that they were supposed to be watching a light romantic comedy, not a hysterically vulgar vaudeville, and so their response to the show was puzzlement when they found themselves hit over the head with appallingly low humor.

Sondheim went back and wrote "Comedy Tonight" – actually the *fourth* opening he had written – and the rest is history.[86]

Even more, Sondheim gives us another perfect GESTALT story in *A Little Night Music*. During that show's out-of-town tryouts, director Harold Prince was working on the scene late in the show where Fredrik tries to tell his former mistress Desirée that he's going back to his wife. Prince told Sondheim that the scene needed a song, and it should be a solo for Desirée. Sondheim objected, contending that it would tilt the scene towards Desirée, and Prince told him that's exactly what was needed at that point in the show.

So Sondheim went home and, overnight, wrote "Send in the Clowns."

And that, class, is how you do GESTALT.

---

86   *Finishing the Hat*, p. 87

links & overlaps

GESTALT goes hand in hand with SUCCESSIVE APPROXIMATION — it is what allows us to see what needs to be changed from one incarnation of our work to the next. Certainly it is the key to *Successful* Approximation.

Just keep in mind that there is no one Perfect Solution waiting out there in the universe for you to bring it to life. There is no Platonic Ideal of your short story or novel or rock album.

That's the good news: you're not stuck with trying to find the One True Solution.

The bad news: what happens if you can't see any kind of path towards the finished product? That happens — a lot, sometimes. If it does, don't keep at it. Maybe it's time for TASK AVOIDANCE or even ABANDONMENT. Come back to it later. With distance, you get perspective. That which sounded or looked amazing last month may reveal its threadbare spots tomorrow.

Or the reverse may happen: that which you banged your head against last month may suddenly show you the way forward by hinting at what it's missing.

GESTALT is also linked to STEAL FROM THE BEST via its *boundaries* aspect: if you're writing a sonnet or a sonata, then that model/structure from the past becomes the guide to your GESTALT. Is the meter of the poetry correct? Have you modulated to the traditional key for the second theme? Or is your GESTALT going to lead you to break past those boundaries and create something new?

GESTALT is where you head when you've run up against that mystery of mysteries, "writer's block." (And of course we include composers, artists, gardeners, coders, and cocktail crafters in the concept.)

―――――――――

Have some pro tips:

Can you take it apart?

Can you destroy it?

Can you whittle it down? Reframe it and work on a fraction of it?

Can you summarize the problem?

Imagine you've decided it's actually finished and ready for an AUDIENCE. As you imagine raising the curtain on it, listen to the voices saying, "Well, except for…"

Go look at Brian Eno's *Oblique strategies*: random instructions that make you think hard – harder than if you were simply working on the project – about where to head next. Two great online versions can be found at http://www.oblicard.com/ and http://stoney.sb.org/eno/oblique.html

Go back to your WASTE BOOKS. What were your impulses to begin with? (Twyla Tharp does this with her project boxes.)

and so...

- Keep looking at the project to see what's *not* there – or what *is* there that doesn't need to be.
- The "shape" of the project *will* change – and that's OK.

LICHTENBERGIAN ANECDOTE

CRAS MELIOR EST.[87]

---

87   That's right. None of the Lichtenbergians came through with an anecdote. Perhaps in time for the second edition...

Precept 5:
Successive Approximation

The thought still has too much elbow-room in the expression; I have pointed with the end of a stick when I should have pointed with the point of a needle.

— GCL, D.18

With many a work of a celebrated man I would rather read what he has crossed out than what he has let stand.

— GCL, F.131

When I was a wee artist attending the Georgia Governor's Honors Program, my teacher Diane Mize took us into the media room and plopped us down on the floor with our drawing boards and pastels. She projected a slide – yes, this was so long ago that this was a daringly high-tech teaching strategy – but it was completely out of focus.

"Draw it," she commanded. We did.

Then she tightened the focus a *tiny* bit.

"Draw it." Working on our base drawing, we continued to sketch. Each time, she would focus the photo a tiny little bit, and gradually huge clouds of color became blobs of color became points of color became recognizable objects.

We built layer on layer of color and detail as the image came into focus, but in the meantime we watched our paper become one piece of work after another. When we went back to the studio, we thought differently about our work there: start it, then fix it. And pay attention to what we've done at each step of the way.

———

All of which is to say – again – that an artist almost *never* produces a finished work; he produces something that is not quite right and then he proceeds to rework it.

The classic gag asks, "How do you make a sculpture of an elephant?" The answer is obvious: "Get a piece of marble and just chip away everything that doesn't look like an elephant." That is easier said than done – of course – but that's the idea behind Successive Approximation. Bit by bit, you make it right-er and right-er.

There are many ways to say it. Fail until you succeed. Fake it till you make it. "How do I know what I think till I hear what I say?"[88]

It's also the point of the Abortive Attempt, isn't it? Just get the thing started: Only begin. Successive Approximation is then the middle ground between Abortive Attempts and Abandonment, passing through Gestalt as it goes.

Artists of all kinds understand this. They employ prototypes, models, sketches, studies, multiple takes in film, theatre or musical rehearsals, jam sessions – all are Successive Approximation. So are scientific experiments, code debugging, focus groups, double-blind drug trials, and if we're being honest about it, the "practice" of medicine.[89]

And the point of all this recursive creativity? Fellow Lichtenbergian Jobie came up with the term *Successful* Approximation for his classroom: every draft, every note, every sketch brings you closer and closer to your final, *perfect* product.

This might be a good time to review your understanding of the word *asymptote*.[90]

---

88 generally attributed to E. M. Forster, but as usual it's more complicated than that.

89 How many times has your doctor said, "We're going to try this [med/procedure]"?

90 An asymptote is a line which a curve (such as a hyperbola) approaches as it heads into infinity – *but which it never touches.*

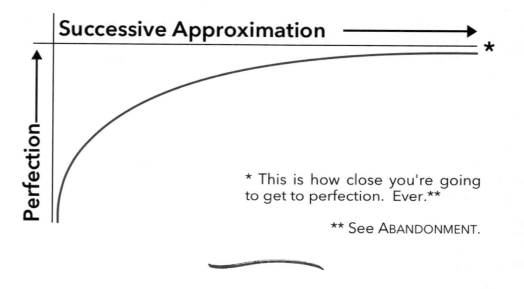

Successive Approximation ⟶

*

Perfection ⟶

* This is how close you're going to get to perfection. Ever.**

** See ABANDONMENT.

One of the key points about SUCCESSIVE APPROXIMATION is made by the fable related in *Art & Fear*[91] of the ceramics teacher who split up his class, telling one half that their final grade would depend only on the *quantity* of their work, i.e., 50 pounds of pots would get them an A; and the other half that their grade would depend on the *quality* of one single pot they produced.

At the end of the semester, of course, it was the students who made *more* pots who ended up with the better work. Every mistake they made along the way was useful, either as a correction or as a new path.

It is like Edison's statement that he hadn't failed 1000 times in inventing the light bulb, he had learned 999 ways not to do it. Each time you attempt a project and fail, you learn something new about the project.[92]

Biological evolution shows the way: every organism is born with slight variations in its genetic makeup. Sometimes the variation is not particularly helpful: a five-legged squirrel might find it *more* difficult to escape the hawk, not easier. Sometimes, though, the mutation helps the individual win out over adversity and permit him/her to mate, possibly passing on the winning trait to

---

91   *Art & Fear* p. 29
92   If you're paying attention. Pay attention.

progeny. If that happens enough, then eventually we might get used to seeing squirrels with hindquarters like kangaroos or elephants with laser eyes.

That's the most important lesson of SUCCESSIVE APPROXIMATION: much of what you make is not going to be a final product. Rather, it's an evolutionary dead end – paint over it, strike through it, use it for firewood. Then do it again. Right-er.

———

Over the years in my various roles as media specialist, artistic director, and educational administrator, I always had to deal with getting things done in an orderly and timely fashion. I had to adhere to (and often develop) processes for these jobs, and in the process[93] I realized a certain truth: "It takes three cycles to get any new process right." In other words, you have to start and end a process at least twice before you can say you have a grip on it. The corollary to the Lyles Theorem of Process Development is, "…if you don't change the process, that is."

That's the whole point to process development, though: you're going to change it. You're going to respond to different inputs and outputs by changing how you deal with them — or at least you *should* be changing the process. If you don't, you risk becoming one of those leaders whose Procrustean policies are despised and resisted by anyone worth having on an effective team.[94]

One of my favorite tools as an administrator is the database application FileMaker Pro. You probably think a spreadsheet is sufficient to keep track of your data: your packing lists or membership rolls or mailing lists. You are wrong. To truly work magic with your data, to control your universe, you need a database.

I've used FileMaker Pro [FMP] to manage every organization I've been in charge of since it came out, and here's why: I can put my data into simple forms, then turn around and output it any way I like. I can slice and dice information and stay on top of things: which theme camps have asked for a space allotment which is clearly too small for their largest object? Which student who lost an Accelerated Reader™ 25-point dogtag has the initials M.H. and got the tag last

---

93 That was a joke.
94 In Greek mythology, Procrustes was a demigod who invited travelers to spend the night. His hospitality was suspect, though: if the guest wasn't the same length as the bed, Procrustes either stretched him or cut off his feet to make him fit.

year? Which season ticket patrons have not yet re-upped their subscription for the new season? Which church choir anthems correlate to the scripture for the third Sunday in May, and when is the last time we performed each of them? I've done all of those and more with FMP.

One example of SUCCESSIVE APPROXIMATION in such a database is that you're not stuck with the information you first put into it. Would it have been useful to know what the largest object in a theme camp was, or the birthday of the members of your theatre company? Create a new field for that info and ask for it next time.

Another way I'm able to use SUCCESSIVE APPROXIMATION to rule the universe is that FMP allows you to "script" its actions, i.e., program the database to perform repetitive actions. So when my wife suggested that the Governor's Honors Program really ought to provide certificates of recognition to every one of the 3,000+ nominees from hundreds of school systems and private schools, I went straight to my database where their nominations were stored.

The thing about scripting (and coding/programming in general) is that you're almost always going to leave out some critical step. Or even if you don't, you will find a way to make it more efficient or cooler as soon as you run it the first time.

So step by step, bit by bit, I built a script that would
1) sort all 3,000 nominees by system, then by school, then by student name;
2) step through each school system,
3) create a PDF file of certificates with the students' names, schools, and areas of nomination on them (using a new layout in the database);
4) snag the email address for the system's GHP coordinator;
5) create an email to the coordinator;
6) write a personalized message to the coordinator; and
7) attach the PDF file.
Whew! Even I was impressed.

The key phrase here is "step by step." I started out with a script that would get the first step done, but after a trial run of the script perhaps something was not right or clean enough and I would tweak that step to make it better: sort by school system, sure, but wouldn't be a kindness to sort each system by school so the local coordinator didn't have to do that? Then I would tackle the second piece and figure out step by step how to do it efficiently and elegantly. Rinse and repeat until finally I was ready to run the whole script for real and generate the hundreds of emails with their personalized messages and attachments.

I could have had the database go ahead and send the email, but I know better than to flood system level educators' mailboxes with trials and errors. Far better to double-check as I hit *send* hundreds of times.

The point is that the database that I built to manage each organization grew over time in its ability to provide me with exactly the information I needed and in a format that was useful.

Not only that, but the whole concept of a database is SUCCESSIVE APPROXIMATION: I used to have a packing list database to help me get ready to go run Governor's Honors for the entire summer; now I have one to get ready to go camp with the hippies at regional burns. In both cases, the database tells me every item I will need and where to lay my hands on it. Also, what I pack and what I leave behind changes every time, and all I have to do is add a new record or delete an old one. Or change a record: if I move the rechargeable flashlights from bin 2 to bin 3, I just make the change in the database. When it's time to get ready, I print out my list (sorted by storage location), gather All The Things, and load up.

As I've mentioned, one of my biggest achievements to date has been setting Nancy Willard's Newbery Award-winning *A Visit to William Blake's Inn* to music. At one point, the Lacuna Group was trying to attract local backing to produce the song cycle as a staged work, and so we decided to stage a "hot glue and cardboard" version of two of the songs from the piece so that those potential patrons with less vision could see "what it would look like."

The group was made up of students and adults of all ages, experience, and talents. Each week we would meet and brainstorm how a static cycle of songs could be turned into action, especially absent a script or plot. Each week we would describe our visions, define problems, and go away to think about them.

And then the following week we would come back with drawings, models, ideas, more and more each week. We'd write all our ideas on pieces of butcher paper stretched across the studio walls; we'd tape our inspirations to them. We'd get on our feet and try out ideas.

We played with themes and metaphors. We invented characters and actions. We added and subtracted based on how the latest addition or subtraction worked.[95]

Every week, the pieces we were working on would take greater clarity and greater detail. I even had to go back to the music and compose a new grand ballet section for our troupe of traveling sunflowers.[96]

Bit by bit, idea by idea, we tweaked and added and subtracted until finally we had a fully visualized staging.

Let's look at what that looked like as we worked on the staging of the song "Two Sunflowers Move Into the Yellow Room," a duet by two sunflowers who tell Blake that "our traveling habits have tired us." We began to envision a troupe of sunflowers, one that we saw periodically throughout the performance, moving from one sunny spot to another, with these two older sunflowers who decide it's time to settle down.

Here's the poem:

Two Sunflowers Move Into the Yellow Room

"Ah, William, we're weary of weather,"
said the sunflowers, shining with dew.
"Our traveling habits have tired us.
Can you give us a room with a view?"

They arranged themselves at the window
and counted the steps of the sun,
and they both took root in the carpet
where the topaz tortoises run.

Here are excerpts from our production blog:

> We played first with the way the troupe of sunflowers moves across the stage the other times we see them. We clumped together upstage right, then moved across the stage in little shifting spurts. [...] I told them, "You keep seeking the sun, the spotlight." Once we get real dancers in there and get them to develop a vocabulary of

---

95   see Gestalt
96   You can hear that at http://www.dalelyles.com/mymusic/wm-blakes-inn/

movement, I think it will work well.

We then entered an intense period of fluctuation: what will the sunflowers look like? We tried baby tutus on our faces as substitute sunflower heads. We had construction paper blooms in our hands. We played with extremely non-dance-like moves. We discussed ways for the troupe to arrive (probably a classical corps de ballet entrance, just swooping in.)

Who were the Two Sunflowers? We keep coming back to their being older, weary of the travel. After their duet, using canonic movement to match the music, we gave them chairs and a small table at which to rest, tea to drink, and probably the Tiger to curl up at their feet.

In the meantime, what to do with the troupe? We kept playing with the idea that tiny movements could mean a lot if you have a lot of flowers on the stage, and with the idea that all the flowers faced the sun, wherever that might be...

And then we had an idea, one of those flashes. Somebody, Marc? Kevin?, talked about making the flowers puppets, in that the dancers would have two sunflowers, one for each hand. The stems would extend to the dancers' feet.

Very quickly, the idea took shape: tubes of green fabric, covering elastic, strapped around the dancers' feet; cloth/flexible leaves; sunflower blooms on handles, so that the heads could rotate independently of the stems. The sunflowers could grow, shrink, turn their heads, talk to one another, and dance.

After establishing the sunflower-ness of the puppets during the duet, then we could let the dancers have more dancer-ish freedom during the waltz, and the AUDIENCE wouldn't think twice about sunflowers whipping about the stage.

Returning to the Two Sunflowers, we decided that the singers too could have a sunflower puppet each, and they could have a leaf that could pick up their traveling bags and teacups.

We're very excited about the Sunflower solution.

Here's where we started:

Young Laura presenting her image of the sunflowers with the traveling troupe in the background.

Carol Lee presenting various options for handling the sunflower puppets.

Molly playing with the first iteration of the crossbar/elastic concept. We began to look at it to see what we would need to do to the basic construction to make it functional and attractive: how long the elastic needed to be, methods of attaching it to the dancer's feet, covering the elastic, materials for the head and leaves, and so on.

Our sunflowers in rehearsal.

And in performance.

When we started, none of us had the end result in our heads. How did we get there? ABORTIVE ATTEMPTS, GESTALT, SUCCESSIVE APPROXIMATION.

SUCCESSIVE APPROXIMATION is just common sense, it would seem. You just have make tweaks and adjustments as you go along. That should be obvious, right? Apparently it's not; for many people, the idea that the first thing that comes out of their head/hand/mouth is not necessarily the finished product is off-putting.

For one thing, it's a lot of work, isn't it? Students all over the world groan aloud when they hear the words "first draft." That means they have to *do it all over again*. Revise. Correct. Expand. It's a lot easier just to plop it out on the page, turn it in, get a bad grade on it, and be done with it.

When I began my career as an educator, I taught English. One strategy I used in teaching writing was to make a list of egregiously bad sentences from the set of papers I was grading, and then the next day write them on the board (this was a *long* time ago) and challenge students to correct them.

Before beginning, I told the students that if they didn't squeak when I wrote their sentence on the board, no one would know it was theirs. The odd thing was that even the kid who wrote the sentence could correct it with no trouble at all. In fact, it was often the student who had written the disaster of a sentence who would immediately offer a perfectly cromulent correction.

The lesson *I* learned was that inadequate writing was mostly a matter of TASK AVOIDANCE: a simple reading out loud of the paragraph would have shown the writer where he went wrong. SUCCESSIVE APPROXIMATION. Bring it into focus.[97]

Scholars of the future are going to face an infuriating problem: authors, artists, and composers of today's digital age will not have left any "rough papers."

In the good old days, those who worked on paper like authors and composers would leave a trail of ABORTIVE ATTEMPTS and SUCCESSIVE APPROXIMATIONS to be pored over by students of their work. Most people don't care about the minutiae of the creative process – who cares how many times Steinbeck rewrote the end of *Grapes of Wrath* – but for those who do care, rough papers are a treasure trove of first thoughts, second thoughts, revisions, rejections, and insights, all of which give us a peek into the artist's creative process.

There's something exciting about knowing "how they did it": which works were a piece of cake, which ones drove their creator crazy, which artists were generally more fluent, which ones constantly second-guessed themselves.

---

97   I wish Lichtenbergianism has been in my toolbox then – instead of the dreaded "rough draft" I would have been able to do what Lichtenbergian Jobie does in his classes: explain ABORTIVE ATTEMPTS and make it all about the process. Even life is SUCCESSIVE APPROXIMATION, isn't it?

Certainly Beethoven sometimes found it necessary to cross out more than he wrote.

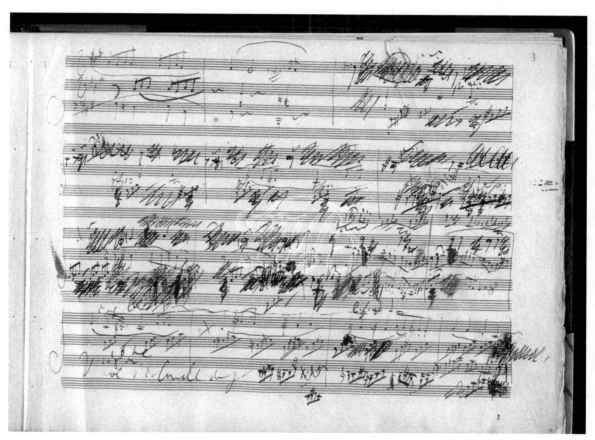

BEETHOVEN'S SKETCHES FOR THE CELLO SONATA, OP. 69

In his WASTE BOOKS we can see eight different beginnings to his Symphony No. 5 in c minor.[98] With each iteration, he listened[99] and found that it was not quite right. That famous theme, the seed, was perfect; the problem he was solving was what to do with it, to lead us, the AUDIENCE, into the complete world of that theme, to make us feel as if what we were witness was graven in stone from the beginning of time – a perfect THING THAT IS.

98   See Leonard Bernstein's examination of Beethoven's SUCCESSIVE APPROXIMATION at https://youtu.be/KI1klmXUER8
99   He was going deaf at this point.

But it wasn't perfect from the beginning of time, was it? This symphony — the very example of what a "symphony" is, what the word "symphony" *means* to the world, the one work that even the least musically literate among us will sing if asked to name a "symphony" — DID NOT SOUND LIKE THAT when Ludwig van Beethoven began to write it.

If Beethoven couldn't get it right the first time, why would you think you should?

links & overlaps

Successive Approximation does not function as a standalone tool, no more than the other Precepts do. Every time you make a change to your piece, you're going to step back and assess whether the change worked or not. That's Gestalt: looking at the whole shape of the piece to determine if anything needs to be added or subtracted.

And of course, every Successive Approximation is a brand new Abortive Attempt. Here's a pretty picture:

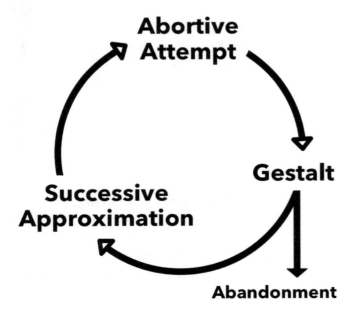

It doesn't get much clearer than this: the King of Hearts Fallacy is a snare and a lie. We MAKE THE THING THAT IS NOT by blundering our way through the cycle of "I'm gonna make some crap" – "Oh crap, it's crap." – "I'm gonna fix that crap" – until finally we get to the off-ramp and ABANDON our work to its AUDIENCE.

Now that you're convinced that you don't have to produce a perfect work straight out of your head, have some Pro Tips for SUCCESSIVE APPROXIMATION:

When I'm writing and I'm going great in a sentence and then all of a sudden I can't think of the correct word or concept or person's name – I will just type XXX and keep going. The XXX makes it easy to see when I'm looking back over a manuscript to see where I just blithely left a blank in the discourse.

When I have beginning and an ending, but not a middle, I'll put in an XXX for the missing section. (This book had *a lot* of XXX's in its evolution!)

If you can't figure out what comes next, *summarize* what comes next. "I need to connect section A to section B." "The melodic line needs to climb to G and prep the modulation to D minor." "The combination of barrel-aged gin, yellow Chartreuse, and Averna Amaro is nice, but it needs a little more spice."[100]

Write yourself questions that you don't have answers to. "What emotion should this section attempt to express most clearly?" "What next step will leave me with several options to move forward?" "Is there a way to embed Theme B in the music at this point?" "Should this section go in the chapter on GESTALT?"

and so...

- The first iteration is not the finished product.
- Do it over, repeat with variations and improvements. Make it right-er. [GESTALT]
- Make it possible to update/upgrade the project.
- Don't wait until you can do it perfectly – dive in. [ABORTIVE ATTEMPTS]

---

100   The Smoky Topaz: 1.5 oz barrel-aged gin, .75 oz yellow Chartreuse, .75 oz Averna Amaro, .25 oz green Chartreuse. Stir, serve either straight up in a coupe or on the rocks in a highball glass. Garnish with orange or lemon peel.

LICHTENBERGIAN ANECDOTE:

CRAIG HUMPHREY: MUSICIAN, WOODWORKER, SHAMAN

Songwriting for me is pretty much just a series of SUCCESSIVE APPROXIMATIONS. These approximations continue until I either get bored with the song and let it wander into the ether or it turns into something that I think other people might actually enjoy hearing. It's no secret to real songwriters that very often the form in which songs end up is not much like what the original inspiration was, but this took me a long time to understand in my own writing.

I was fortunate enough to have a good bit of time one year to work almost exclusively on two things that I very much enjoy and find creative — cabinetmaking and playing/composing on guitar. (I use the term composing with trepidation lest anyone think that I actually know what I'm doing.) During this time, I played a chord progression for a friend who gave me some positive feedback and the progression kept coming back. Gradually, through SUCCESSIVE APPROXIMATIONS, the progression began to turn into something that wasn't very much like the original idea at all. It became something a little more connected to my persona and, as such, a little more what I think creativity is — a revelation of some aspect of who we are, if just for a relatively brief time. More SUCCESSIVE APPROXIMATIONS yielded verses, iterations yielded choruses, and collaboration yielded a bridge. I was finished! Except for how I didn't really like that phrase, and how that line was so clearly borrowed from another musician. Crap! Time for more approximations.

After playing around with this song for a year on my own and another two years with a band, it finally became something I'm reasonably happy with. It's my second favorite song on our recording and I think it holds up OK under repeated listenings. I rarely have had the patience to stick with a song for the length of time this one required and go through the SUCCESSIVE APPROXIMATIONS necessary to let the song emerge from the original inspiration. I'm glad that this is one time that I did.

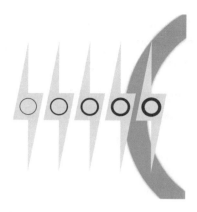

Precept 6:
Ritual

Perhaps the roof-tiler fortifies himself to meet the perils of the day through a morning prayer, and if so he is among the fortunate; perhaps, however, he does it with a portion of baked cat's brains. Oh if only we sometimes knew what gives people courage!

— GCL, J.114

When I was translating *The Marriage of Figaro* for performance at the Newnan Community Theatre Company, I was still mid-career as an educator so my time was limited. I discovered that the best way to get my thinking/rhyming/lyricist cap on was to play *Dreamtime Return*, Steve Roach's New Age double album. That first track — with its insistent rhythm and never-quite-clear melodic fragments — was enough to trigger my brain into the liminal state, wherein it was open to the trials and tribulations of translation: plot, characterization, clarity, singability, rhyme, and punch lines. I should probably be playing it right now to help with this chapter.

Of all the Precepts, RITUAL is probably the one that gets the most quizzical looks. That's because for many the word evokes secretive meetings of villainous individuals up to no good, or conversely, something grand and glorious involving cathedrals and incense.

Or for some, the word conjures up an empty set of repetitive practices, drained of all meaning and performed only because that's the way we've always done it.

Let's rescue the word.[101]

RITUAL is a kind of structure, one that takes you from where you are to a new place, crossing over a line in some way to get there. Its purpose is to provoke change in yourself and/or the AUDIENCE. You find the structure in any religious service, in the Hero's Journey,[102] in all the superstitious little ways artists will arrange their work space and time to make that transition into a state of "work-mind."

Once you understand the way RITUAL works, you can use it to make your creative work more meaningful and actually easier to get at.

Take a look at this outline:

- Invocation
- Drawing the circle
- Taking the path
- Numen/Connection
- Breaking the circle
- Benediction

Looks awfully religious, or at the very least pretty hippie-woo, doesn't it? There are those who would say that creation — the act of MAKING THE THING THAT IS NOT — is a spiritual act and hence sitting down to write the next chapter of your romance novel is analogous to Sunday morning at First Presbyterian. I do

---

101   NERD ALERT: The study of RITUAL has been one of my major interests over the last decade, and the topic is rich and complex. This chapter, alas, is going to be a bit thicker than the others, mainly because it takes more explaining. Trust me, I've rewritten this chapter three times. My apologies in advance.

102   See Appendix C: The Hero's Journey

not disagree with them. Both the writing and the church service are RITUALS with a shape and a purpose, and that purpose is to change the person who engages in it. For us as artists, that change is moving from the chaos of the universe to a bit of the universe that is perhaps a little less than chaotic.

Let's get down to concrete examples.

First, a picture of the shape:

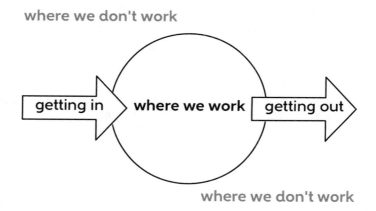

where we don't work

getting in — where we work — getting out

where we don't work

That's it, really. The next several thousand words just explain it.

Invocation

Invocation comes from the Latin meaning to "call upon," and at First Presbyterian it means literally calling God in to be a part of the gathering. J.S. Bach did exactly the same thing when he scrawled *JJ* at the top of every new manuscript: *Jesu Juva – Jesus, help me!* When literature was still a direct reflection of the oral tradition, back in the days of *The Iliad* and *The Odyssey*, you can see it as well: *O Muse!* the poet pleads. *Help me tell this story!*

For us mere mortals, though, it's more a matter of calling upon our own attention and energies. Art doesn't happen just because. It happens because we *will* it to happen. We must *decide* to MAKE THE THING THAT IS NOT, and that requires that we need some kind of call to our own brains to get to work and to stop worrying about getting the herb garden planted or what to pack for the weekend.

Recognizing that we have to enter into the circle to do our work is the first step to overcoming our fear of failure.[103] You might very well create your own actual **Invocation** that you use to get started, but all that's really necessary is developing a sense that you have a switch that you need to flip from OFF to ON.

Let me be clear that I do not mean that you turn your *creativity* on like a space heater. That's not how it works. Rather, **Invocation** is like turning the lights on in your studio as you get to work. It's an announcement to the universe that you are ready to enter that space where you MAKE THE THING THAT IS NOT.

Once you've done that, then the rest of it is a piece of cake, right? Sure, it could happen.

I will share with you the literal **Invocation** that I wrote and actually use when I'm starting a major project.[104] If it's a group project, I will read it out loud to the assembled group. If it's just me in my study, I still invoke the spirit of the inimitable Ed Wood.[105]

Invocation

O Ed Wood,
We beseech thee,
O Edward D. Wood, Jr.:

Look over us now as we begin our new masterpiece.
Blind us to the possibility of failure.
Hide from us the improbability of our success.
Free us from our capabilities,
and strew our paths with bad ideas,
so many that we cannot help but stumble
upon a good one every now and then.

Give us the clarity of vision
to see as far as the next step before us,

---

103   Failure is always an option. *see* ABANDONMENT.
104   Yes, this is the same as Appendix B.
105   If you're not already a fan of the irrepressible Mr. Wood, go watch his *Plan 9 from Outer Space*, followed by Tim Burton's *Ed Wood*. It will renew your faith in the human spirit.

but not so clear that we fail to see our own genius
rushing forth like a river and covering all about us
with an ever-rising and brilliant flood of success.

Grant us this, O Ed Wood,
now and in the hour of our rebirth.

Selah.

Drawing the Circle

Drawing the Circle is the next step. Once you've invoked your muse or turned on your lights, it's time to set your space. For most of us, that means closing the door in some way: protecting your time and concentration so that you're not interrupted by spouses or children or pets or Facebook (!).

Arrange your desk, set out your drawing materials, sharpen your pencils, set your word count goals. Do some practice scales, review yesterday's orchestration, proofread yesterday's chapter. Ask your big question, set your sights, gird your loins.

What you're doing is entering what students of RITUAL call the liminal space: you cross a boundary from the "real world" into a space where change is not only possible but practically inevitable. (Why else would you willingly enter it?) Religious RITUALs sometimes even make the boundary a real one; they draw a literal circle for the liminal space, and when you come out of the circle you are now a man, or healed, or married.

Drawing the Circle can also mean setting aside a specific time for your work. Nowadays I blog first thing in the morning, after checking email and social media, followed by work on the book or on music, followed by lunch, and then in the afternoon I can run errands, or garden, or exercise, or write letters, or read, or volunteer, or other stuff. (Yes, I am retired; why do you ask?)

When I was *not* retired, my time was more restricted, of course, as I'm sure it is for you. I found that I was most productive by setting aside specific nights for composing/writing and making very sure that the other nights were open to family and friends.

I've always been fascinated by artists like Jane Austen, who is said to have written her perfect novels on the fly, whenever she could grab a moment. She didn't closet herself in her study or head out to her personal writing cabin;

when she went to Bath, it wasn't on retreat. If someone came into the room while she was writing, she would slip her papers into the drawer and rise as if nothing were going on.

It may sound as if she was able to switch her creativity on and off, but I think the actual deal was that she **Drew the Circle** in a different way because she had to. She created her workspace in her head: during all those long walks, or household duties, or quiet evenings at home, she was working on Miss Elizabeth Bennet and Mr. Darcy in her interior writer's cabin. Scribbling on her foolscap was just stenography.

The point is that whether you have your secluded cabin that you go to every weekend to write your next symphony or you have to scribble your novel on envelopes as you walk the dog every morning and evening, it's up to you to **Draw the Circle** to create your liminal space and then — deliberately, willingly — enter into it to MAKE THE THING THAT IS NOT.

Taking the Path

We've turned on the lights in our studio, we've arranged our materials. We've thanked and welcomed whatever muse has shown up — if any — and now it's time to do the work.

Let me take a moment to explain why the outline of the structure of RITUAL is worded the way it is. These terms are the sections in a blank book I've created for myself for my labyrinth in my back yard, collections of wisdom from poets, philosophers, mystics, and hippies that I can use in my personal meditations.

It's as lovely as it looks.

So **taking the path** is a literal thing for me as well as a metaphor. Let's look at the metaphor.

The purpose of any RITUAL, as we've already said, is to offer the possibility of change to the participant. For that change to happen the participant must leave Point A and take the risk of change by traveling to Point B. For many of us, the fear of that risk is what

A 7-CIRCUIT LABYRINTH

keeps us from beginning the journey at all. That's where the Precept of ABORTIVE ATTEMPTS is so incredibly useful: it helps us ignore or at least minimize that fear by saying, essentially, "This first step on my journey doesn't count."

In a nice circular way, RITUAL helps you make that first ABORTIVE ATTEMPT by showing you how to take that first step along the path. Note, too, that the complete journey means that you return to Point A before you're done. If we compare this part of the RITUAL to the Hero's Journey,[106] we can see that we will encounter the struggle of our own creativity while on this journey, and that upon our return we hope to have been victorious, bringing back our new creation as a gift to the world.

That's a lot of philosophy flopping about here when all we really mean is that you have to take the trip, do the work, risk the change in your work — and in yourself — in order to MAKE THE THING THAT IS NOT.

But I think it's useful philosophy if it helps you think of your *fear of beginning* as a normal part of the process. You don't know what you will encounter on the path. You never know. But after your **Invocation**, after you've **Drawn your Circle** — take that first step. **Take the Path**. Walk the labyrinth.

Go to the wood! Just don't expect to be home before dark.

Numen/Connection

In my *Book of the Labyrinth*, I've named this part of the RITUAL structure **Numen/Connection**. It's actually two sections in the Book, but for our purposes we can combine them since both involve an encounter.

First of all, what is **Numen**? It's a Latin word meaning "divine power," and we're going to use it to mean that indefinable quality of our creative process that we don't always understand — it seems to come from beyond us, from the universe at large.

Some call this *inspiration*, and that's an interesting word too because it comes from the Latin meaning "to breathe into," and the implication is that it is a deity doing the breathing into us. Think Jahweh and Adam. The old hymn "Breathe On Me, Breath of God." The Oracle at Delphi. Someone who is *inspired* is obviously in touch with **Numen**.

---

106   You should really go read Appendix C.

Alas, the Romantics skewed our understanding of *inspiration*. Most of us these days think of artists as tortured souls who simply *can't even* until they are *inspired*, and then they pour out their art in one rushing torrent of beauty and perfection.

This is ridiculous. As in, I will ridicule this concept every time I come across it. Art really doesn't work that way; not even John Keats would tell you that, and he was as tortured as they come.

Here's a more useful concept: as you're working, as you're **taking the path** – listen. Stay open to the two equally important channels of **Numen** and **Connection**. **Numen** is both the universe at large and your innermost voice. Listen for ideas that seem to come from nowhere. Follow your impulses.

For example, when I was working on my *Six Preludes (no fugues)*,[107] I started the first prelude with a ferocious theme that tumbled headlong down the staff like a downhill skier on a steep slope. As it approached the two or three measure mark, I told myself that it was probably time to wind the theme up and begin working out its possibilities.

However, that's not what happened. I stopped myself from stopping and just listened: the theme kept going – seemingly by itself – all the way down to the bottom of the bass clef. All in all, the theme made itself into a six-measure-long monster and gives the listener the impression that there's no time to even to take a breath as it plunges on and on beyond reason. It was so striking that I used it verbatim as the end of the piece. So much for my rational planning.

Listen to what the universe is suggesting. That's **Numen**.

Despite my pooh-poohing the Romantic notion of *inspiration*, in which the artist writhes in personal agony until his Muse arrives to touch him and breathe into him his ideas and his genius – which I still insist is poppycock – I will confess that there are parts of the creative process which simply cannot be explained.

Especially when we are fabulously successful at our art we may find ourselves wondering, "Wait – I did that? How? When?" Pieces of the puzzle appear and fit snugly and we have no idea where they came from.

Most of my music is so hard-won that I know *exactly* where it came from, but occasionally I will finish a piece and realize I have no memory at all of the work I did to finish it. Take, for example, the second theme of "Prelude No. 3 (no fugue)." It's a series of long, calm chords which break up the first theme's rushing stream of sixteenth notes: I probably did those chords on purpose, as

---

in "I need something to let the AUDIENCE breathe and the pianist's fingers take a break."

But the ideas that start at m.24 are not mine: I am not clever enough to combine the stream of sixteenth notes with the second theme, and then to have the climax be that calm second theme transformed into something exultant. I have no memory of making that work.

It does work, though. At the two performances of the *Six Preludes* that I've heard, AUDIENCES have applauded the third prelude, despite conventional concert etiquette requiring they wait until the whole suite is over before politely clapping. They think they're applauding me (and/or the pianist), but I know they're not. It's a mystery.

Sometimes, then, our creative work comes from a source that seems to be outside ourselves. I'll accept that. The smart money, though, is on preparing ourselves (via RITUAL: **invocation**, **drawing the circle**, **taking the path**) to be open to **Numen**, because – trust me – the Angel of Art is never going to come handing out freebies all on his own.

The other channel we must be open to encountering is **Connection**, and a good synonym for that is our very own Precept of AUDIENCE. As you work, *connect* to your AUDIENCE. Include them in your work.

This does *not* mean that you are limiting your grand, soul-inspired work to what might appeal to mere paying customers, as it were. If that were the case, I'd never have written most of my music or my blog posts. (Or this book.)

But when you're working, you are never working just for yourself. You are working to MAKE THE THING THAT IS NOT so that it can take its place in the universe with the rest of us, and for that to happen, you need to *offer* it to the rest of us (or at least a subset of the rest of us), and we should be a part of your work. Stay connected.

Let me wrap this up by returning to the overall structure of RITUAL and its relationship to the Hero's Journey. After the Hero crosses the threshold into adventure, he will encounter forces beyond his understanding or control. He must deal with them in some way, either by allying himself with them or engaging them in struggle. He may not succeed, but he must engage if he is to be in any way successful in his quest.

And so it is with us: we must engage with powers that we don't fully comprehend – inspiration and AUDIENCE – because if we don't, then we don't create art.

Breaking the Circle

Now let's talk about getting out of here.

Soon enough, it's lunch time, or time to walk the dog, or you're doing some weird time management thing, or maybe, just maybe, your brain stops working. (It could happen.)

It is entirely possible just to lay down your pen/brush/cocktail shaker and walk away. Who's going to stop you? It's probably a better idea, however, to **break the circle**, i.e., to formally acknowledge that you're done.

More than a few writers advise stopping when you're actually doing well: don't wait until you run out of ideas. Stop when you know exactly the next thing you're going to write. That way, when you next enter the circle, you are not staring at the blank paper with the same lack of ideas you left it with.

side note: This is the same principle behind my advice to actors learning a long monologue or to singers learning a new piece of music: start at the end and work your way backwards. That way you're always heading into material you know (which you then reinforce) rather than constantly running into a dead end of stuff you haven't learned yet (and learning the *stopping* rather than the *continuing*.)

In general, the "quit while you're ahead" gambit is good advice. You end on a positive note, and you will not dread getting back to work as much.

But even if that's not what happens — because let's face it, who wants to quit when you're on a roll? — and you end up at Level 7 on the Lyles Scale of Compositional Agony,[108] take the time to say to yourself and to the universe, "I'm done here. I'm going to be doing the ABANDONMENT thing for a spell. Be right back."

Clean your brushes. Save your files. Tidy your desk. (It could happen.) Organize All The Things.

Take a step back.

Take a deep breath. Stretch.

Now go empty the dishwasher.

---

108   See Appendix D.

Benediction

And here we are. We've laid down our pen, our brush, our cocktail shaker. We're done. Calloo! Callay! We chortle in our joy.

Just as **Invocation** is as simple as making sure to flip the light switch on, **Benediction** is simply acknowledging you're done.

In addition to turning the lights off, you should probably throw in a little gratitude there, as well as a promise to return. The universe likes that kind of thing. Might make it easier next time. (Spoiler alert: it will not make it easier.)

If you've stuck with this section, you may be thinking that the whole thing seems a bit overwrought. It sounds as if you need bell, book, and candle just to sit down and write a love poem. TOO MUCH WORK!

It's really not, though. Go back to that simple diagram:

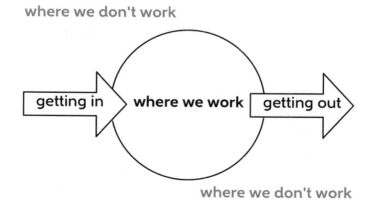

We use RITUAL to move from Where We Don't Work into the circle, into the liminal state, Where We Work. That's it.

Another name for the liminal state is *flow*, named and popularized by Mihaly Csikszentmihalyi in his book of the same name. He discusses consciousness and how we manage ours, specifically in situations in which we find ourselves completely engaged in what we are doing and therefore, presumably, happy.

Most artists will tell you that when the work is going well they have no sense of time or effort: that is *flow*. They will also tell you that when they say there's "no effort," it doesn't mean they're not constantly working out kinks or dead ends — it's just that they find excitement in the working out instead of frustration.

Thus the history of creative types is full of all the ways we have triggered that working/liminal state of mind. Ernest Hemingway and Virginia Woolf stood at their desks to write; Mark Twain and James Joyce wrote lying down. Victor Hugo wrote naked (mostly to keep himself from leaving the house). German poet Friedrich Schiller kept rotten apples in a desk drawer, claiming that the smell helped trigger his creativity.

RITUAL can be pretty damned impressive. Every year, on or before the winter solstice, the Lichtenbergians have their Annual Meeting, which you will encounter in full in the chapter on AUDIENCE. Short version: we meet around the fire on or before the winter solstice. There is a set Agenda, which among other things requires us to state our Proposed Efforts for the coming year and to confess whether or not we were successful in avoiding the completion of the previous year's Efforts. (*Cras melior est.*)

For most of us, though, simpler RITUALs suffice. We need time, space, materials, and commitment, and RITUAL can help us meld all those things together. You can use it on a daily basis to make it easier to cross over that line into the *flow state*. By acknowledging that you're willing to get to work — **Invocation, Drawing the Circle** — you trigger your brain/soul to enter that liminal space where the words or notes or ideas come from.

It doesn't guarantee success, of course; sometimes you eat the Minotaur, sometimes the Minotaur eats you. But unless you open the door and enter the labyrinth — **Take the Path** — you will never encounter **Numen**, you will never make the **Connection**. You will have a very hard time indeed MAKING THE THING THAT IS NOT, and it's hard enough as it is.

Make it easier: **draw that circle, take that path**.

It is important — it is really important — that you not think of RITUAL as something involved or complicated. You don't have to break out the smudge stick every time you want to write a poem. That's not the way it works.

And there's not a "right" way to do it. Check out Mason Currey's book *Daily Rituals* for a look at how scores of writers, musicians, and painters have structured their approach to their work. Some work(ed) at the same time every day, like regular office hours — and even then some worked first thing in the morning while others worked at night. Others waited until the "pain of not writing exceeded the pain of writing."[109] Examine how others have done it. Steal From the Best if one Ritual approach strikes your fancy — or just know that if the great artists all had different ways to get into the circle, you are free to follow your own path to the center.

My personal Ritual for getting into the circle is mostly *where*, not *when*. I work best in my usual spots. I am a creature of habit — and that habit is Ritual.

I work in my study, of course, but I also work in my comfy chair in the living room and in my Adirondack chair by the fire pit in my back yard. Those three places seem to invite my focus: study, living room, back yard.[110]

However, not all three places are equivalent. The living room chair and the fire pit are usually my Abortive Attempt locations: jotting down ideas, scribbling first drafts, mapping out plans. Or I'll retreat to them for editing, for Successive Approximation. The study is where I get most of the "real work" done, fleshing out the drafts, pounding out the musical ideas, etc.

Again, through my work habits, they have become Ritual spaces. When I need to plan, I go to the living room or the fire pit depending on the weather, and my brain enters that liminal state. When I'm past the Abortive Attempts stage, I close my Waste Book and exit the circle.

Likewise, once I'm ready to hammer my ideas into shape, I'll head up to my study, spread out my plans, open whatever software I need, set my timer, and get to work.

I think that when you're working with a group Ritual becomes even more important. One of the functions of Ritual is *communitas*, the creation of a group bond: a congregation will bow their heads in prayer. A court session begins with everyone rising for the judge's entrance. The great Ritual of Burning

---

109   Too many writers have said something like this to give a single citation. It must be true or something.

110   My back yard, of course, was designed to be a place of meditation and concentration, so that's not a stretch.

Man begins with the Golden Spike being driven into the desert ground at the location of the Man — and the rest of the city layout springs from there.

I've mentioned my Ed Woods "Invocation." I will also, when directing a play, begin every rehearsal by gathering the cast in a circle and leading group warmups — stretches, vocalizations, etc. I make it clear that this time is not for chatting or chattering; it is time to focus your mind and energy on the work we're about to do. We are literally entering the circle. Outside the circle is homework, cranky family, frustrating jobs — inside the circle is our space to build the world of *King Lear* or *The Odd Couple* or *The Marriage of Figaro*.

linkage & overlap

The Precept of Ritual undergirds pretty much the entire Lichtenbergian structure.[111]

The practice of Task Avoidance/structured procrastination is a Ritual: a way to manage your work deliberately while pretending to avoid it.

Waste Books are themselves a Ritual: a structure for turning ideas from the vaporware in your head to something a little more concrete in this world.

Recognizing the cycle of Abortive Attempts/Gestalt/Successive Approximation and approaching it deliberately is a Ritual: it's a shape that you use to Make the Thing That Is Not.

and so...

- Find the time and space that suits your working habits and needs, then protect them.
- Find a pattern that leads into (and out of) your liminal space.

---

111   Since I believe Ritual undergirds most of life, this is not surprising.

LICHTENBERGIAN ANECDOTE:

Back in 2009, the Lichtenbergians set themselves an Assignment: list your Five Rules for Creativity. What we got from everyone consisted of lists of RITUAL behavior.

Here are mine:

1. Start every venture with the words "ABORTIVE ATTEMPTS" at the top of the page.
2. Face up to the fact that quantity is better than quality — and more likely in the first place.
3. Make your distractions as productive as your work.
4. Defend your time.
5. Learn to look/listen for what is missing.[112]

It was interesting that some variant of "Defend your time" appeared on everyone's list.

What are your Five Rules?

---

112   You will notice the presence of the foundations of Lichtenbergianism even then.

Precept 7:
Steal From the Best

To discover relationships and similarities between things that no one else sees. Wit can in this way lead to invention.

> — GCL, I.9

To do the opposite of something is also a form of imitation…

> — GCL, D.96

Everything that has happened will happen again. Everything has been done and will be done again. There is nothing new under the sun.

> — Ecclesiastes 1:9

Several years ago I was inspired to take up painting again. My focus was on the nature of my medium (gouache/artist colors) and on compositional balance. One day I came across a photograph from the late 19th century, the composition of which appealed to me.

I printed it out, glued it to a board, and began to paint over it, using the photographer's image as a template for my brush. At every step of the way, I used GESTALT and SUCCESSIVE APPROXIMATION to evaluate my new work against the original, until finally I reached ABANDONMENT: I was done.

The painting looked nothing like the original photograph, although I imagine if you're familiar with the original you will recognize its bones beneath the layers of paint:

I then went on to create a series of paintings using the same strategies as this one: small, indistinct figures, sometimes black, sometimes colors, eroding their way through a heavy field of white paint. Now, however, they were my own original compositions.

I "stole" the photograph to learn what I needed to learn.

FIELD SERIES NO. 1 (2009)

Artists are supposed to be astonishingly original, aren't they? You MAKE THE THING THAT IS NOT, and the AUDIENCE is dazzled by something they've never seen before, right? So we have to ask: as an artist, why would you steal from anyone else?

As famous bank robber Willie Sutton famously never said when asked why he robbed banks, "Because that's where the money is."

The Precept derives from the saying, "Good artists borrow; great artists steal," often attributed to Pablo Picasso. (According to the Quote Investigator,[113] the saying has a more complicated history, none of which lessens our lesson here.) In its various incarnations, the message is simple: we take from those who have come before and use their gift to us to create our own THING THAT IS NOT. Merely borrowing what came before, however, is not enough; the new THING may be *good*, but it cannot be *great* unless we have taken it completely as our own and left nothing behind.

Using Picasso himself as an example, let's look at his breakthrough 1907 painting *Les Demoiselles d'Avignon.*[114] Students of art history will already know that the faces of the two women on the right were inspired by African masks[115]. A "good" artist might have seen the masks and included them in a painting without changing much at all. The masks would remain as they were, untouched, and the painting would remain solely as a record of the masks.

Instead, Picasso saw the masks and "stole" them for his own purposes. He incorporated the angular planes and the slashes and the stark colors into his burgeoning Cubist style – and the result is that the masks he saw are gone. His *Demoiselles* takes us forward into something new – shows us a new world – and now we look back at the masks in a different light.

Good artists borrow; great artists steal. If we are going to steal, let's STEAL FROM THE BEST.

113   Good Artists Copy; Great Artists Steal. (n.d.). Retrieved November 17, 2015, from http://quoteinvestigator.com/2013/03/06/artists-steal/
114   http://www.moma.org/collection/works/79766
115   http://masks.novica.com/

So from whom do we steal, and how?

First of all, steal from the past. The past has left us a treasure trove of forms and models and patterns, and it behooves you to study them. Look at the sonnet, the sonata, the Golden Ratio, the Hero's Journey, the rule of thirds, iambic pentameter, the fugue, the recipe for a Manhattan cocktail – all are there for your consideration. Anything that has proved useful in the past is still useful.

Whatever your chosen area, go back to its roots and use its forms and models. Even if they are "passé" you will still gain from the structure they provide. And no one says your final product will end up adhering strictly to the old rules. For example, the structure of "Blake Leads a Walk on the Milky Way," from my *William Blake's Inn*, is essentially in the sonata allegro form.[116] Bear with me: this gets technical.

As practiced by Mozart and the gang, the first movement of a symphony, a concerto, or a sonata was in the *sonata allegro form*, which had three parts:

Exposition		Development	Recapitulation		
Theme A	Theme B	all kinds of keys and modulations	Theme A	Theme B	Coda
main key (tonic)	related key (dominant)	and interesting stuff	main key (tonic)	main key (tonic)	

1. Exposition: we hear two themes (musical ideas, melodies) – **Theme A** and **Theme B**. **Theme A** is in whatever key you needed it to be, and then **Theme B** changes to the *dominant* key, i.e., a fifth above. (Don't worry about getting this: just know that Theme B was in a different key than Theme A.)

2. Development: the composer takes those two themes and plays with them: uses pieces here and there, changes keys, combines them, does all kinds of tricks to entertain us. Finally, we are led back into the…

3. Recapitulation: we go right back to the beginning with **Theme A** in the original key, followed by **Theme B**, this time in the original key as well. We end up with a coda, a little "tail" that finishes it all up.[117]

I decided that "Milky Way" was a natural for the sonata allegro structure because Nancy Willard repeated the first two stanzas at the end of the poem, but

---

116 http://dalelyles.com/mymusic/wm-blakes-inn
117 Savvy readers who have read Appendix C like I told you to in the last chapter may recognize the shape of the Hero's Journey in the sonata allegro: call to adventure, struggle, return.

I futzed with it: since the first two stanzas of the poem were repeated in reverse order at the end, I reversed the order of Themes A and B in the recapitulation as well. Not only that: although Theme B appears after the development section in the "correct" key of A minor, Theme A finished out the work in C major, which is not outrageous but not where it was "supposed" to end up.

It might not get me an 'A' in a Composition 101 class — probably none of my music would — but it works.

You might very ask how I know all this if I've never been trained as a composer. That's my point: no one gave me this knowledge — I stole it. I stole it from textbooks and encyclopedias and album covers. I stole it from choral directors. I stole it from Mozart and Beethoven and Prokofiev.[118]

It's there for the taking.

Steal from your culture.

Steal from the world at large.

Steal from nature.

And finally steal from artists whom you admire, both past and present.

Here are some ways to do that legitimately:

Emulate your heroes. Learn to play their music. Read their books. Study their paintings. Make their cocktails.

Reverse engineer their work — figure out how they did it. Use the same strategies they used, but to create *your* work. Even today you will find art students in museums, doing their best to copy the great masters, or musicians learning the great guitar riffs from classic songs, or bartenders following classic recipes. They're learning the possibilities of their craft.

To return to Picasso, go find his takes on Velázquez's *Las Meninas*.[119] He did *fifty-eight* paintings replicating all or part of the old master's group portrait, each time exploring a bit more of it and making it his own. As he put it, "...what if you put them a little more to the right or left? I'll try to do it my way, forgetting about Velázquez. The test would surely bring me to modify or change the light because of having changed the position of a character. So, little by little,

---

118   Want to hear a super-clear lesson in sonata allegro form? Check out the first movement of Prokofiev's Symphony No. 1, "Classical," which he wrote when he was 17 as a graduation exercise at the conservatory. It's a perfect example of the form. (It was also a thumb in the eye of his professors — he was already chafing at the strictures of academic formality and he wrote it just to show that he could do it. Then he never looked back.) http://imslp.org/images/8/82/PMLP04505-01.I.Allegro.mp3

119   https://en.wikipedia.org/wiki/Las_Meninas_(Picasso)

that would be a detestable Meninas for a traditional painter, but would be my Meninas."

Picasso got it. So did Cy Twombly, who did the same thing with Raphael's *The School of Athens*. So did I, with my first "Field Series" painting.

Austin Kleon wrote an entire book on the topic: *Steal Like an Artist*, a taut little treatise on being creative. He covers many of the Precepts,[120] concisely and wittily, and he's adamant about pillaging the past. Be a packrat of ideas and techniques, especially of those artists you admire.

As he says, "The great thing about dead or remote masters is that they can't refuse you as an apprentice… They left their lesson plans in their work."[121]

The point is that you do not have to start from scratch — and no one expects you to.

I'll share some more examples of my theft.

Between the second and third movements of Beethoven's *Emperor Concerto*, there's a held note that then drops a half step as the composer leads us into the new key and new landscape — I've used that one weird trick multiple times in various works.

The "Prelude No. 4 (no fugue)" was written as a deliberate homage to — if not an outright theft from — Dmitri Shostakovich.

In one of the more amusing thefts of my career, I translated Mozart's *Marriage of Figaro* for my final production as artistic director of the Newnan Theatre Company. We performed the glorious finale of Act II at the season gala in January to demonstrate to our small-town AUDIENCE that yes, the show in October would be fun and, even better, it would be funny.

When we got to Figaro's entrance, two of the company who were in the wings watching suddenly burst into raucous laughter. Afterwards I asked what was so funny, and they said that they realized I had stolen Figaro's opening melody for my own "A Reason for Laughter" in *A Christmas Carol*, which they had just finished performing. I had forgotten doing that, but in a flash I remembered

---

120   None of this is new. Ecclesiastes was right.
121   *Steal Like an Artist*, p. 17

thinking, back in 1980, that no one in Newnan would ever make the connection. Hoist on my own petard, indeed.[122]

These few examples are mostly *ad hoc* thefts. Here's one that's more deliberate and strategic.

One of my ongoing Lichtenbergian goals for the past several years has been a piece called *SUN TRUE FIRE*.[123] It is based on a surprisingly long spam comment I once got that is weirdly poetic and just beyond any literal meaning.

I intend to work several years on the piece, and this is the manner of my working:

- Examine the text and make notes on what kind of music I think will be best for it
- When I hear a piece of music that sounds like something I would like to have written for *SUN TRUE FIRE*, make a note of it and which text I would have applied it to.
- Write a passage of music based directly on the target — see if I can create something that produces the same effect with similar strategies/structures.

This is purely stealing. Specifically, it's *parody* in an older sense of the term: using the structure of one work to create another. Nowadays, parodies for the most part are satiric, mocking either the original work or using its familiarity to mock something else in the public consciousness.

But not all modern parodies are jokes. Michael Cunningham's novel *The Hours* is brilliantly structured, almost stroke for stroke, on Virginia Woolf's *Mrs. Dalloway*. In fact, Woolf is a character in one of the plot threads.

In a less artistic endeavor, E. L. James' *Fifty Shades of Gray* began as fan fiction based on Stephenie Meyer's *Twilight* novels. Talk about an ABORTIVE ATTEMPT!

I'm only halfway joking there — you can see how using the parody/modeling concept is a good way to get your own ideas solidified. After James' fiction found an AUDIENCE, she applied a little SUCCESSIVE APPROXIMATION to her unpublishable (because of copyright) work and *voila!* the next thing she knows, she's outselling J.K. Rowling.

---

122   Even earlier, I had stolen the entire sextet at the end of Act II for the grand finale of my one act opera version of *Green Eggs & Ham*, which was never granted copyright clearance by the Seuss estate and so remains unperformed.

123   *see Appendix E*: SUN TRUE FIRE

So look around. Find something you admire. Futz with it. Layer your own work on top of it. Create something new that may or may not make it clear that you have a source.

As Lacuna Group was workshopping its way through *William Blake's Inn* back in 2007, we had two sets of rules that we posted on the wall and followed. Here's the first set:

1. **Be nice.**

   This one is self-explanatory.

2. **Ollie-ollie-oxen-free**

   Can be invoked when some are hiding opinions or even disapproval from the group out of fear of looking stupid. When invoked, some kind of round-robin sharing is required of everyone.[124]

3. **Reader's Digest**

   Can be invoked when a speaker is being complex or obtuse and confusing people. When invoked, the speaker must give a simple summary of what he/she just said.

4. **Fail.**

   Remember that the group consisted of seasoned if not leather-hided creatives like myself plus those who were considerably younger and/or less experienced. It was the first time for most working on a performance where they had to devise that performance. The rules guaranteed that everyone felt safe to contribute: there were no stupid ideas.

At that same time, I stumbled across another set of rules that we adapted. Apparently (for I am no mathematician nor a historian of mathematics) there were two famous British mathematicians, G. F. Hardy and J. E. Littlewood, who famously collaborated on a lot of famous math stuff. Before they began their collaboration, which they did almost exclusively through written correspondence, they decided to formulate some rules which would protect their "personal freedom."[125]

---

124   "Round-robin" is a classroom technique, also known as "whip around": you go around the circle and everyone has to contribute their thoughts on the topic.

125   Whatever that means.

The first of them said that, when one wrote to the other, ... it was completely indifferent whether what they wrote was right or wrong ...

The second axiom was to the effect that, when one received a letter from the other, he was under no obligation whatsoever to read it, let alone to answer it ...

The third axiom was to the effect that, although it did not really matter if they both thought about the same detail, still, it was preferable that they should not do so.

And, finally, the fourth, and perhaps most important axiom, stated that it was quite indifferent if one of them had not contributed the least bit to the contents of a paper under their common name ...[126]

Applying our **Reader's Digest** rule:

1. We don't worry about whether what someone else has said or done in work is "correct" or "good" or "bad" or not.
2. We don't have to respond to or engage in an idea or work or post that does not interest us or we do not understand. (Although, of course, we do have an obligation under the **Ollie, ollie oxen free** rule.)
3. It is better if we're not all thinking the same thing as we work. Another way of translating this is to say that everyone needs to share their ideas.
4. As we commit to a piece of work as a group, it is irrelevant who thought of it first or who contributed the most.

Not only did we steal from Hardy and Littlewood, we set ourselves up to steal from each other.

In the past, it was taken for granted that artists would borrow and steal from each other. Part of this was the lack of copyright protection – about which more in a moment – but mostly it was a healthy approach to the international trade in ideas. J.S. Bach's *Concerto for Four Harpsichords* is his transcription/remix of Antonio Vivaldi's *Concerto for Four Violins*, and of course Bach was known to cannibalize his own work for new pieces. In turn, Bach's Prelude in C Major from *The Well-Tempered Clavier* was remixed by Gounod for his *Ave Maria*.

Then there are all those "Variations on a Theme by [insert composer here]": composers honored their predecessors by playing with a melodic line that

126   From the collected works of Harald Bohr, quoted by Bela Bollobas in the foreword to *Littlewood's Miscellany*, Cambridge University Press, 1986.

appealed to them, sometimes in the style of the original but more often in the modern composer's own style that may have been largely incomprehensible to the theme's original author. In Rachmaninoff's *Rhapsody on a Theme of Paganini*, the theme doesn't even appear in its full form until after the first variation. The showboating Paganini would have been flummoxed, although he surely would have approved of the virtuosic nature of the piano part.

Today, of course, copyright law has restricted the use of much of the immediate past. The original intent of the 1790 law in the U.S. was to protect the creative artist's right to income from his/her original work *for a limited time*, after which the work was released into the public domain, where it was available for anyone to use. This served two purposes: *1)* it kept a steady supply of good stuff we could all use flowing into the commons; and *2)* it nudged the artist to keep creating new good stuff so he could keep getting paid for it.

Since the Copyright Term Extension Act of 1998, though, copyright obtains to a work until 70 years after its author's death.[127] Copyright protection extends to permission to create *derivative works*, i.e., something made *based on* an original work: my musical version of *William Blake's Inn*, the novelizations of *Star Wars*, Bach's *Concerto for Four Harpsichords*. Because of this aspect of copyright law, even parody (supposedly protected as fair use) can be problematic. (Examples of lawsuits claiming infringement in today's sample-heavy hiphop culture are not hard to find.)

So while Bach had an easy time of it, understand that you as a modern artist can't literally *steal* someone else's work to pass off as your own. Just like the plagiarism you learned about in high school term papers, copyright infringement is illegal.

It's also bad art.

links & overlaps

Use your WASTE BOOKS to STEAL FROM THE BEST: by scribbling and jotting, you can get down exactly what you want to steal and why. (That's what I'm doing with *SUN TRUE FIRE*.) Work your way through those ABORTIVE ATTEMPTS before

---

127   This will amuse you: once I was considering entering a choral music contest and decided that for my text I would use the ancient hymn, *A Elbereth Gilthoniel!* It was with some shock that I remembered that it was not an ancient text, it was copyrighted literary fiction – J.R.R. Tolkien's poetry from *Lord of the Rings* – and that it wouldn't be out of copyright until 2043.

committing to the theft, and then perhaps it won't even be theft when you're ready to move on it.

When you're stuck in GESTALT, puzzling over what's missing or what's wrong with your work, ask yourself, "What would [your favorite artist] do?" Give yourself the gift of someone else's brain.

and so...

- Don't be afraid to emulate your heroes.
- Stuck? Look for how others have solved it — and try it yourself.
- Learn and use the great forms of the past.

LICHTENBERGIAN ANECDOTE:

MARC HONEA: THEATRE ARTIST, POET, MUSICIAN

I published a daily haiku on Facebook for almost an entire year. My motive at first was rather self-serving and somewhat self-ennobling. I needed to assert that I was unsoiled by the sometimes sordid social media stream I religiously forded each morning while sipping my coffee. So I chose a form that was, to my mind, inherently ennobling: one that would allow me to dispense with the vagaries connected to the quest for inspiration or with wondering whether or not I possessed sufficient inner richness and linguistic cleverness to produce poetry in the first place and, instead, focus on simply rising to the dignity of what is there, of bearing witness. And I chose a form that was manageable: all I had to do was attend to my world and my impressions and then render a few each day in seventeen syllables. People of Facebook, behold my restraint, my lack of indulgence, my Zen-like emptiness, my brutal grasp of what's really there...

So, to steal some attention and respect, I stole a form. I thought, in appropriating the form, I was guaranteeing myself a certain bit of credibility, of status, of inflation. I would cynically fulfill the formal requirements and attention would be mine by right. That's not what happened, of course. A noble form, after all, ennobles. A form endures because of what it calls forth from both artist and audience. Like the criminal disguised as a Lord in Kurosawa's *Kagemusha*, I was transformed by the act of imitation. And so was my work.

Precept 8: Audience

It is almost impossible to write anything good without imagining someone, or a certain group of people, whom one is addressing. In 999 cases out of a thousand it at any rate greatly facilitates the execution.

— GCL, L.76

"To possess is [necessarily] to give."[128]

— Lewis Hyde, *The Gift*

I was at an event where an artist friend, Keith Prossick, was showing some of his paintings,[129] and I overhead a conversation as I passed by one of his works. It was a larger painting, and the brush style was a little looser than most of his work. Apparently that prompted a young man to ask whether the painting were finished, to which the young woman standing with him said, "Keith always says the painting is never finished until someone buys it and takes it home."

Keith says he always adds, "...or until I die." Either way, a work of art is not complete until the AUDIENCE is given a shot at it. Think of these two artists: Emily Dickinson and Vincent van Gogh. Neither was well known in their lifetimes.

---

128   *The Gift*, p. 283
129   http://keithprossickarts.com

Emily wrote mostly in secret and in fact left instructions to burn her work after her death. Vincent sold almost none of his canvases before he died.

In both cases, a sibling rescued the work and then made it their business to make sure that the world — the AUDIENCE — saw it. Without that AUDIENCE, Emily Dickinson's poetry would be a pile of ashes; Vincent van Gogh's *Starry Night* would be landfill. Don't leave the work to your siblings. Share your work with your AUDIENCE now. Let us in.

———

Who is your AUDIENCE?

I can tell you who your AUDIENCE is *not* by reminding you what the authors of the excellent *Art & Fear* tell their readers: the Museum of Modern Art [MOMA] is not your AUDIENCE.[130]

The *New York Times* bestseller list is not your AUDIENCE.

The Tony Awards committee is not your AUDIENCE.

Austin Kleon, author of *Steal Like an Artist*, said in a tweet one day (and I'm paraphrasing from memory): Imagine yourself appearing before an adoring crowd of hundreds, even thousands of fans. Do you imagine that every single one of them really, truly cares about your work? No, of course not. Maybe half a dozen do. *Those people* are your AUDIENCE.[131]

I would add: The rest of them are The Crowd.

Don't create for The Crowd. The Crowd has no taste. The Crowd will throw money at you — for a while — but The Crowd is fickle. The Crowd will desert you as soon as something new and different comes along.

Create for your AUDIENCE.

Let's talk about your AUDIENCE, or rather, your AUDIENCEs. You have at least two:

1. *Those people* out there.
2. *Those people* right here.

The first AUDIENCE is that great, invisible crowd of people to whom you will eventually ABANDON your work. They're the ones who will read your book, listen to your music, stroll your garden, review your research. If there are enough of them, they may very well propel you to that bestseller list or that Tony Award,

---

130   *Art & Fear*, p. 12
131   Kleon also wrote *Show Your Work*, which is entirely about AUDIENCE.

but even so they are not infinite in number. You are not MAKING THE THING THAT IS NOT for everyone.

Let me say that again: your work is not for everyone. It is for your AUDIENCE. Even our top earners know this. Stephen King is more successful at his writing than I could ever hope to be, but he does not write for me – horror fiction is not my *frisson*. And he knows that. When he's working on his next book, he is not thinking about how to please people for whom horror is a horror.

Likewise, Philip Glass is not writing music for those who prefer a thumping bass – I am not creating cocktails for those who like sweet, fruit-juice drinks – and Michael Bay is not making movies for people who appreciate plot and nuanced characters.

Take Kleon's advice to heart: who are those half dozen souls in the screaming throng who truly grok your work? Create for them.

———

Then there's your second AUDIENCE: those people right here.

If you've done any reading about your favorite artist, you will have noticed a peculiar thing: *all the cool kids seemed to know each other.*

Elizabethan London, Renaissance Italy, the Enlightenment, the Lost Generation, the Cubists, the Beats, the Abstract Expressionists, the Harlem Renaissance – on and on – the stars of those groups all knew each other. They were all together there at the nexus of art being made.

How does that happen? How do all the famous creators fall into the same circle?

Part of the answer is that they create those circles and those circles in turn create them. Musician Brian Eno, when he was an art student, began to look askance at the way artistic giants like Picasso and Michelangelo were being presented as solitary men of genius, towering alone over their time and place. He, too, saw that they were part of the cool kids club, and he devised a term for that: *scenius*.

He defined *scenius* as "the intelligence and the intuition of a whole cultural scene. It is the communal form of the concept of the genius."[132] It is Those People Right Here.

———

132 *A Year with Swollen Appendices.*

As blogger Kevin Kelley puts it, a scenius gives its members "mutual appreciation, rapid exchange of tools and techniques, network effects of success, and local tolerance for the novelties."[133] When you're surrounded by people inspired by the same things as you, you all benefit from the flow.

You may recall from the "Introduction to Lichtenbergianism" that the

> **"People after the same self-discipline as yourself, following the deeper commitment... A bond like that with other people is in itself an ecstasy."** — *Flow*, p. 42

Lichtenbergian Society was founded almost by accident. It was a spur-of-the-moment invitation from me that brought us together on that Solstice evening — and it was a random quote from Turff that set in motion the founding of this ridiculous excuse to drink around the fire. Within this fellowship — and there is no other word for it — we are free to discuss our art, or politics, or our personal lives, or each other's personal lives, and that creates a *space*, a refuge, a retreat — and that space is our *scenius*: AUDIENCE. (I'll talk more about how that works in a moment.)

I joked on my blog that I could scrap this entire chapter and instead tell you to read *Bandersnatch: C. S. Lewis, J. R. R. Tolkien, and the creative collaboration of the Inklings*, by Diana Pavlac Glyer. She distilled her much more scholarly *The Company They Keep* into a extremely readable account of the Inklings that only seems to be a detailed study of how members of the group interacted and influenced each other — in fact, it is as good a treatise on scenius as you are like to find.

She calls members of such groups *resonators* and says that they "show interest [in the work], give feedback, express praise, offer encouragement, contribute practical help, and promote the work to others."[134] She then proceeds to give specific examples of how the Inklings did each of these.

In the penultimate chapter, "Leaf-Mould and Memories," she expands the concept to include our very own STEAL FROM THE BEST: you are wise, she says, to include the great creators of the past in your influences. And her last chapter is an epilogue on How To Do What They Did, i.e., create your own scenius: start

133 http://kk.org/thetechnium/scenius-or-comm/
134 *Bandersnatch*, p. 30

small; stay focused; meet often; embrace difference; start early and intervene often; criticize but don't silence; vary feedback; increase the channels; try more than one; and think outside the group.

As I said, detailed and complete.

———

There is actually a third AUDIENCE: yourself.

Think about it: as you work through the cycle of ABORTIVE ATTEMPTS, GESTALT, and SUCCESSIVE APPROXIMATION, you are trying to please *your* eye, *your* ear, *your* sense of wholeness and completion. Only *you* can decide when it's time to ABANDON the work.

Once again, MOMA is not your AUDIENCE. None of the artists whom you admire, not even the ones who are filthy rich, create their work for some abstract notion of fame. It is certainly true that Those People Out There will give you money for your work — I will have no objections if this book sells a million copies — but the surest way to short-circuit your process is to stop listening to you inner AUDIENCE and try to hear instead the fickle and nonexistent voice of The Crowd. Stick to your inner AUDIENCE; if it also pleases MOMA or the bestseller list, that's great — remember to invite me to your private Caribbean island for a stay — but never pursue an AUDIENCE that *does not exist.*

Most artists are in fact their toughest AUDIENCE. Even today when I hear some of my music, I can hear all the compromises, the splices, and the outright failures to achieve what I thought I wanted from the piece — but almost no one else can.

The trick is to be your own AUDIENCE, not your own Critic. There is a difference.

So, be your own AUDIENCE for your work-in-progress. Use morning pages or some kind of journal (WASTE BOOK) to chronicle your efforts. Blog about it if you like. Nothing clarifies the mind like putting your failure out there for all the internet to see.[135]

One strategy I use at Backstreet Arts[136] with anyone who "thinks they might like to write" but don't really know about what is to hand them a WASTE BOOK and tell them: Imagine you're on The Late Show with Stephen Colbert to talk

---

135   http://Lichtenbergianism.com
136   a local arts studio for homeless and other underserved populations: http://backstreetart.org

about your book. He asks you, "So, [name], what made you want to write about [XXX]?"

I tell them to write the question down in the WASTE BOOK: "So, [name], what made you want to write about [XXX]?" They do that. "Now answer it," I say, and they look at me oddly and try to talk about it, but I simply say, "You're a writer on a talk show, being asked about your work in front of millions of people. What is your answer?"

They'll work for a while and finally come up for air. Invariably they will want to read it to me, but I tell them, "Look, now you know *what* you want to write and *why* you want to write it. So write." They cock their head, their eyes widen, and the lightbulb clicks on.

Especially if you're stuck, journaling can be very helpful. Ask yourself questions or define what it is you're trying to do. That will help freeze-frame all those fuzzy ideas swarming your brain like so many gnats. (See GESTALT.)

For example, here are some notes from a WASTE BOOK on an unfinished poem of mine entitled "341: Georgia's High Tech Corridor." The idea sprang from a drive down to Georgia's coast along Highway 341, where I was startled to see an official road sign proclaiming the absolutely rural highway to be Georgia's "High Tech Corridor."

I wrote five stanzas, setting the scene in sestets of heroic couplets, and then bogged down because although I had very strong images of the situation, I hadn't really been able to define what it was I wanted to say about them. Here's what I scribbled in the WASTE BOOK:

> So what are the ways in which we [me and my family] are free that differ from the HTC?
> – connectedness to a larger world
> – insularity of rural areas
> – distrust of the Other, of newness, of people who are more educated, more sophisticated?
> BUT what's the point?
> Maybe I'm just grateful not to be a part of the limited world, having come from such a place myself.
> So the solution to not appearing to scorn the innocent (?!?) inhabitants is to turn the focus of attention on myself – explore why *I* fear and distrust this milieu

Now I have focused my projector a little bit more; parts of the picture are clearer. *How* I'm to finish the poem is still a blur, but now I can speak more clearly to my AUDIENCE: myself.

I have come to believe that it is the AUDIENCE-as-*scenius* aspect of the Lichtenbergian Society that has proven crucial to our successes despite our joking commitment to TASK AVOIDANCE, and it is the RITUAL of the Annual Meeting that embodies that aspect the most.

Every winter, on or before the solstice — the darkest day of the year — we meet around the fire in my back yard, and we have an Agenda:

1. Roll Call
2. Toast to GCL
3. Acclamation of the Officers
4. Corroboration of the Validity of our Claims
5. Consignment of the CORROBORATIVE EVIDENCE to the Flames
6. Engrossment of the Year's Efforts
7. Meditation on the Year's Efforts, followed by the Burning of the Coals & a Silent Toast
8. Censure for Betrayal of the High Ideals of the Society
9. Engrossment of the Proposed Efforts for the Next Year
10. Toast to the Proposed Efforts
11. Topic: "Lichtenbergianism: a Thing or What?"[137]

We draw the circle with our roll call and our Toast to G. C. Lichtenberg, and then we have some dead serious business: Corroboration. Our whole philosophy is based on procrastination — *cras melior est* — and so we look askance at artists who have not learned to procrastinate quite enough, putting out into the marketplace that which perhaps ought to have been postponed instead.

Each year, at least one of us brings a sample of CORROBORATIVE EVIDENCE to share with the group, and then we burn it. Privacy concerns (and fear of litigation) prevent me from sharing with you the artists whose work we have

---

137   The Agenda from our Annual Meeting in 2014

consigned to the flames, but of course the world provides no shortage of such stuff.[138]

Then the core RITUAL of our Society: the Engrossment[139] of the Year's Efforts, followed by the Engrossment of the Proposed Efforts for the Next Year. (I'll come back to Censure in a moment.)

The Secretary has a big record book, the hardbound, blue kind you see at office supply stores. In it, in his indecipherable handwriting, he has listed what we said would be our creative goals for the year at the previous Annual Meeting. He now reads out by the light of the fire each goal, and the member in question has to discuss how he met the goal – or didn't.

If he didn't, then the appropriate liturgical response is a simple *Cras melior est* – I'll get to it.

We each confess our successes and failures, and then we have a silent toast over the fire. We also, as we meditate on what we accomplished over the past year, toss the coals we took from the previous fire into the flames.

And then the Secretary is ready to Engross our Proposed Efforts for the coming year.

The effect of this RITUAL has been pretty amazing. When you know you're going to have to sit at fireside and discuss how and why you did or did not achieve your stated goals, it makes a difference in your commitment.

It also makes a difference in the goals you set. One year I achieved every single goal – and that was *not* a good thing. Were they too easily achieved? Had I *cheated* in setting them? Whatever the case, it certainly seemed to me – and to my fellow Lichtenbergians – that I had failed to live up to the lofty objectives of the Society.

It was not better the following year when I hadn't achieved *any* of my goals. The fact that had I achieved a respectable number of non-goals was irrelevant.[140]

That ceremony, that RITUAL, requires us to present our Selves as Accomplished. We must drop the pretense that we're not "really" artists and instead proclaim what we want to work on in the coming year. We must bind ourselves to our fellow Lichtenbergians in a trust that demands that we regard our creative impulses as legitimate – and not merely impulses, but imperatives.

---

138   One year I tossed in one of my own ABORTIVE ATTEMPTS, a pieced called *Earth Dance* for low strings and percussion because I realized I had ripped off Jimi Hendrix's *Purple Haze*.

139   Engrossment: the final version of a legal document, which is ironic considering that our annual statements of intent are anything but definitive.

140   Other than being the entire point of TASK AVOIDANCE, of course.

Within the confines of the Lichtenbergian Society, failure is commendable and success is to be deplored — at least that is our comfortable pose. Of course we are actually proud when one of us publishes a book or finishes a musical work or gets his Equity card, or even — to cite one recent example — to become a proficient "corporate tool."

But around the fireside, at the Annual Meeting, these successes are a matter of some concern, holding as they do our founding principles as naught. Especially egregious are those successes that go beyond our small circle and attract the attention of the world outside the fire. It is one thing to write a short story that no one but the group will read — it is quite another to have a book signing at Barnes & Noble.

We therefore have incorporated Censure as a part of the Annual Meeting's Agenda — if a Lichtenbergian has not only achieved an annual goal but has gained fame from it, no matter how moderate, then he must explain himself to the group.

Yes, it's all tongue-in-cheek, a way to recognize our members' accomplishments — but it also gives us a framework within which failure to achieve is a perfectly acceptable option [see ABANDONMENT]. Within the circle, in fact, failure to achieve makes you a member in better standing than anyone who actually succeeds.[141]

And that is why I think it works — without our scenius, we would be creating our work with nothing between us and Those People Out There. The fear of failure, the certainty of no reward (or worse, ridicule) would be enough to turn us all into permanent procrastinators, afraid to make even the smallest ABORTIVE ATTEMPT. Within our scenius, we are free to fail — *encouraged* to fail — and like the pottery students in *Art & Fear* we have ended up producing far more successful work than we otherwise would have.

As noted previously, the sceniuses of the past are both legion and legendary, far too many discuss in detail here.

One of the most famous was The Inklings, the group of Oxford University writers who met every week during the 1930s and 40s to read aloud their

---

141   Trust me, I shall not escape Censure once this book is released.

unfinished works and invite comments and criticism.[142] They met in C. S. Lewis's rooms on Thursday nights, but they would also meet for lunch on Tuesdays at the local pub The Eagle and Child, aka The Bird and Babe.

It was here that J. R. R. Tolkien read portions of his new sequel to *The Hobbit*, and it was famously said (by C. S. Lewis) that he had only two reactions to criticism of the piece, either to ignore you or to scrap what he had written and start over. As for influencing each other, Lewis said that "no one ever influenced Tolkien — you might as well try to influence a bandersnatch."[143]

For a scenius you might not have heard of, check out *February House*, by Sherill Tippins. The book's subtitle is "The Story of W. H. Auden, Carson McCullers, Jane and Paul Bowles, Benjamin Britten, and Gypsy Rose Lee, Under One Roof in Brooklyn," and that's as good a synopsis as I could give you. Back in the late 1930s, all these creative minds ended up sharing a brownstone in Brooklyn, and Tippins' chronicle of their output is fascinating. It's enough to make you want to start your own commune.[144]

links & overlaps

As stated at the opening of the chapter, AUDIENCE is the end of the circle.[145] After all, either we ABANDON the work to an AUDIENCE, or we're just ABANDONING it to the trash heap.

I mean it: anything you don't end up sharing with an AUDIENCE is not art. As I've always told any writers with whom I've worked, the purpose of poetry is not to express your emotions; the purpose of poetry to get *other people* to experience those emotions. After all, was Emily Dickinson actually dead when she wrote "I heard a fly buzz" or "Because I could not stop for Death"?[146]

Share your work.

---

142   See Glyer's *Bandersnatch*, referenced above.
143   Glyer gives a more nuanced and complete understanding of this comment, p. 131-132.
144   There is also, incredibly, a musical based on the book.
145   Is that a koan? Or just a borked metaphor?
146   https://www.poets.org/poetsorg/poem/i-heard-fly-buzz-465 and https://www.poets.org/poetsorg/poem/because-i-could-not-stop-death-479

and so...

- MOMA is not your AUDIENCE.
- Find or create your scenius.
- Be your own AUDIENCE: journal your efforts in some way.
- Solve problems/roadblocks by describing what the problems/ roadblocks are and why they are what they are.
- Announce your projects, even if it's only to yourself.
- Keep a record.

LICHTENBERGIAN ANECDOTE:

JOBIE JOHNSON: TEACHER, WRITER, THEATRE MAKER

In the realm of who is your audience (those people out there, these people right here, yourself), let us return to Greg Allen's 7th rule[147] for creating good theatre: **Rule #7: Know your audience. Have some idea whom you are creating the show for. Firstly it should be for yourself. But secondly it should have some target for whom will be in the audience – children, teenagers, punks, the rich, the old, liberals, grad students, women, gays, a specific ethnicity, etc.. Theater "for everyone" is bland theater.** If your concerns are the concerns of the DACA recipient, do not write a piece trying to explain to someone what it's like to be a DACA recipient: write your piece for the DACA recipient. Narrow your focus, narrow your audience. If the message is massaged into something for "anyone" to understand comes off as pedestrian at best, proselytizing at worst. If you speak directly to the narrow audience though, refusing to contextualize what you don't feel the intended audience needs contextualized, refusing to footnote who Sauron is but going into great detail about the evolution from Melkor to Morgoth in a book about fantasy-book lovers (looking at you, Junot Diaz), then your audience may not have the cognitive experience of "understanding" the "meaning" of a piece, but the piece's sincerity and earnestness will transcend.

---

147 http://www.neogregallen.com/greg-allens-26-rules-for-creating-good-theater/

Precept 9: Abandonment

Never before had a mind come to a more majestic halt.

— GCL, C.3

Let's let the grass grow over it.

— GCL, I.2

In 2015 I was directing my musical version of *A Christmas Carol* at Newnan Theatre Company. I wrote the piece back in 1980 and the company had done it nearly every year for 20 years, but after I left the position of artistic director it fell into disuse. However, everyone at the theatre remembered it fondly and so they asked if I would revive it. I said sure.[148]

Somehow, in the intervening years, all the costumes we had built up for the show had mysteriously disappeared, so we had to rebuild. My stage manager and I pulled over 100 items from the shop for cast members to try on, so you can imagine my surprise when — a week before we opened — I was told that almost *none* of the costumes fit the people we had.

If you're a theatre practitioner, you will understand that I didn't panic; I just pivoted to Plan Z: triage, simplify, and dragoon people into sewing the absolute

---

148   History has been compressed and diluted in this account to protect the innocent.

necessities. In this case, I needed four 1860s-style hoop skirts; a plethora of cravats; and five Empire gowns. Everything else we'd patch together.

Mrs. Fezziwig was a seamstress, so I gave her the hoop skirts: waistband, pleated skirt, go. The boys and I whipped out the cravats. And I called my good friend Jennifer Schottstaedt[149] – an amazing costumer and actress – to ask if she could do one simple thing: make five identical Empire bodices, sized to the actresses, and we'd attach the gathered skirts ourselves.

The day before we opened, I got a call from Jennifer: she was way behind and freaking. Not a problem: if she'd bring everything and her sewing machine down, we'd all pitch in. When she arrived, I saw the problem: instead of whipping out five identical bodices, she had designed five entirely different, complete gowns. Gorgeous, of course, but not ready to be worn.

And so we worked for the next 24 hours helping Jennifer finish these beauties, finally shoving her out the door at 7:30 as we opened the house to let our AUDIENCE in.

Were the dresses finished? If you are a theatre practitioner, you know the answer to that: of course not. That's what safety pins are for.

It's time to turn to ABANDONMENT.

Sometimes, you just have to stop. You have to walk away from the work. You have to stay away from the work.

Sometimes, you just have to stop.

The deadline has passed.

You've worked yourself into a corner.

There is no further impetus – or AUDIENCE.

You run out of steam.

The GESTALT no longer reveals itself.

You're done. It's finished. It's time to let the AUDIENCE have it.

ABANDONMENT can mean several different things to the artist. You can, as the Valery quote on the next page suggests, stop working on a project and declare it finished – or you can throw it away – or you can just stop working on it for the time being, i.e., TASK AVOIDANCE.

> "A poem is never finished, merely abandoned." — Paul Valery

---

Is the ABANDONMENT permanent? Who's to say? Sometimes you think a project is dead, only to find that its purpose is revealed later; or a phrase you discarded as trite or saccharine or otherwise cringe-inducing somehow finds a new purpose in a different work altogether. It happens more often than you think.

(That's one reason ABORTIVE ATTEMPTS is such an important Precept – if you generate a lot of material, you will have that much more to go back to, to fall back on, to rummage around in.)

But what if it is permanent? What if your project is over, dead, trashed? What if you actually have to ABANDON it?

Remember what the Lichtenbergian Society says about it: "Failure is always an option." The whole structure of Lichtenbergianism, of this book, is to give you the tools to fail, to fail often, and to fail upwards.

The thing is, the Precept of ABANDONMENT reconfigures the entire concept of failure. It's part of the process. "Failure" implies that you did something untoward, that if you were a *real* artist you would have ridden that wave all the way to the shore and shaken the sun-kissed ocean drops from your California hair, or metaphors to that effect.

This is nonsense. You have not failed, you have ABANDONED work that is longer your work. *Real* artists know this. As I always told parents of the 3,000 students nominated to GHP when they asked what if their child were not one of the 700 finalists, "Not all baby sea turtles make it." Not all art gets finished.

No, it's not fun. Yes, it's painful. But ABANDONING your work doesn't make you less of an artist; it makes you more.

In his book *Little Bets*, Peter Sims hammers home the point that ABANDONMENT must be embraced if you and your team want to "fail quickly to learn fast." You can't, he says, cling to the first idea you come up with, nor stake everything on what seems like a sure bet.

Giving examples from stand-up comics to Pixar to Frank Gehry to Barack Obama's 2008 campaign to Muhammad Yunus's microlending Grameen Bank, Sims shows how ABANDONMENT is both natural and necessary to the creative process. Stigmatizing "failure" is itself a failure to understand how organizations – and artists – grow and thrive. Churn, contained chaos, flexibility: these are the hallmarks of a healthy creative team.

Sims is not alone in suggesting that letting go is essential. Nearly every author referenced in the bibliography agrees: when an idea or project is not working out, it's time to set it aside. If the idea is going to work, you can return to it later; if not, then it's best to move on.

Here are some things I've Abandoned:

- the opera *Seven Dreams of Falling* – playwright Scott Wilkerson and I hit it off right away when introduced by a mutual friend. He churned out the libretto for "Dream One" and I spent a lot of 2014 working on it. Then his Ph.D. became a task he couldn't avoid, and I got sidetracked by other things, and neither of us has circled back to it. It's still on my Big List. *Cras melior est.*
- the Epic Lichtenbergian Portrait – soon after I picked up my brushes and began painting again, I conceived the idea of doing a group portrait of members of the Lichtenbergian Society. I worked for quite a while beefing up my life drawing, did a whole series of studies, and then just stopped. (But I'm using many of those images in a current small art project.)
- the "341" poem – I mentioned this poem in the last chapter; here's the full disclosure: it's been years since I've worked on it. I'll probably never finish it.
- the chapter on RITUAL: I have trashed two previous versions of the chapter you skipped three chapters ago. (You didn't? Good for you!)[150] I just straight up threw them away as I found better ways to say what I had to say. Likewise, I wrote three different introductions to this book and then picked one.

I could go on, but you get the point.

150   But did you read Appendix C?

You may recall way back in the chapter on ABORTIVE ATTEMPTS that the Lacuna Group had worked on a devised performance piece about being a creative adult male in a milieu that didn't necessarily value that, and that we eventually stopped working on it.

Here's another group experience: a couple of years later, a couple of us wanted to re-enter that collaborative space where we created *Coriolanus*, and so we decided to play with *King Lear*. We worked in exactly the same way, meeting once a week just to delve deeply into Shakespeare's text, each of us playing different roles in randomly selected scenes.

We developed some really interesting images and strokes, and I even came up with the intriguing approach of disassembling the script and putting it back together all out of order: we'd start with the storm scene, then flashback to the opening, and then leapfrog back and forth in time watching the storylines progress in an almost whodunit kind of structure.

But for whatever reason, we never finished it. We didn't have enough people, and real life kept intervening. We ABANDONED it.

The architect Frank Gehry builds models of the buildings he's designing, over and over and over, each iteration improving/fixing the one before. If he feels stuck at any point, he tells his team, "Let's let it sit there and annoy us for a while."[151] ABANDONMENT in the service of GESTALT.

J. R. R. Tolkien stopped working on *Lord of the Rings* multiple times, once as long as a year and a half. Part of this was his lack of time, but mostly it was because he worked slowly and methodically. He was constantly fiddling with his subcreated world of Middle Earth and its mythologies, languages, and geography, and sometimes he just didn't know what came next in the story. He ABANDONED Frodo repeatedly in order to give himself time to work out the details: ABANDONMENT as SUCCESSIVE APPROXIMATION.

Harper Lee wrote *Go Set a Watchman* in 1957, and although the publisher J. B. Lippincott bought it for publication, Lee's editor Tay Hohoff[152] decided that it needed some work, to wit, toss it out and rewrite it to focus on the young girl's childhood experience instead of her adult self reminiscing. The result of course

---

151   from the documentary *Sketches of Frank Gehry*, https://youtu.be/vYt2SQPqTh0
152   You *wish* your name were Tay Hohoff.

was *To Kill a Mockingbird*, the staggering American classic, the direct result of ABANDONMENT.

Stephen King – young, married, and poor – was desperate to sell more of his writing. He wrote the draft of a short story, took a step back from it, decided it wasn't working, and literally threw it in the trash. His wife found it, read it, and convinced him to get back to work on it. He did, but it became too long for a short story. He was forced to turn it into his first novel, *Carrie*. ABANDONMENT when it should have been ABORTIVE ATTEMPT.

German artist Anselm Kiefer, already mentioned in the chapter on TASK AVOIDANCE, has raised ABANDONMENT to be the central pillar of his creative process, leaving works behind for years while he works on other things. With him, it could be said that his work cannot be considered to be ABANDONED until he dies.

Then there's Post-Impressionist painter Pierre Bonnard, who was so obsessed with perfecting the colors in his work that he convinced his friend Éduard Vuillard to distract the guards in a museum so he could touch up a painting he had "finished" years before. Don't be that guy.

links & overlaps

ABANDONMENT links to TASK AVOIDANCE: many a project gets set aside for whatever reason and may take a long time to bubble back to the top of your kanban pile. It may never come back into play, but TASK AVOIDANCE is, in the main, at least temporary ABANDONMENT.

Finally, on a positive note, ABANDONMENT also applies to success. When you finish the book, the song, the painting – you're done. What else is there to do but ABANDON it to the AUDIENCE? Who but artists can describe the feeling they get when they are done with their work as ABANDONING their "baby," a sinking feeling in the pit of their stomach as they send their creative effort to face the tender mercies of the very people it was created for? Hi ho, the glamorous life!

and so...

- Give yourself permission to stop — it's OK to stop gnawing at it.
- Let it go — walk away from it and come back later to look at it. [GESTALT]
- Failure is a perfectly acceptable option.
- Be interested in your failures. Make them interesting.
- It's also perfectly acceptable to succeed.

LICHTENBERGIAN ANECDOTE

CRAS MELIOR EST.

The Tenth Precept

We do not think good metaphors are anything very important, but I think a good metaphor is something even the police should keep an eye on...

— GCL, E.91

There is no tenth precept.

The great festival Burning Man operates on what its participants call the Ten Principles. They are:[153]

1. Radical Inclusion
2. Gifting
3. Decommodification
4. Radical Self-reliance
5. Radical Self-expression
6. Communal Effort
7. Civic Responsibility
8. Leaving No Trace

---

153   http://burningman.org/culture/philosophical-center/10-principles/

9. Participation
10. Immediacy

Take the time to look them up and read about them. They tend to change your life, especially if you actually attend a Burn operating in accordance with them. Like Lichtenbergianism's Nine Precepts, they're loosely defined and organized, but somehow they create a coherent whole.

But you know hippies — once you've given them the Rules, they're going to mess with them. Almost immediately, the arguments began for one or another "11th Principle." The frontrunner these days is "Consent," i.e., don't touch, gift, or photograph another hippie without consent. (In Temporary Autonomous Zones like Burns, sometimes it's easy to forget that not everyone else is your kind of freak.)

So *should* there be a Tenth Lichtenbergian Precept?

Sure, why not?

After we held the Lichtenbergian seminar at GHP back in 2013 and I began to consider creating this book, I also began to wonder whether the Precepts were all-inclusive: did they cover all the bases of the creative process as embodied by the experience of the Lichtenbergian Society?

It seemed that every time I found a blank area, the Precepts actually reflected both the theory and practice not only of the Lichtenbergians but of other systems of the creative process as well. I specifically went through Twyla Tharp's *The Creative Habit*, for example, and outlined the main precepts of her book in order to map them to Lichtenbergianism. Everything fit, one way or the other, with nothing left over and nothing left out.

Still, there have been concepts that I was tempted to install as our Tenth Precept before deciding they were probably already there as part of one of the others. You might consider them as your own Tenth Precept.

The strongest contender was BOUNDARIES: knowing where the fences are, then going beyond them. Making yourself strike out into Wallace Stevens' jungle and tame it. To invoke another of Stevens' images, place a jar on a hill in Tennessee and force everything to align itself in relationship to that jar. MAKE THE THING THAT IS NOT.

I finally decided that GESTALT would include the idea of BOUNDARIES, but your process might require more recognition of what your limits supposedly are and the necessity of breaking through them.

PATTERNS was next. It ended up in GESTALT as well (and partly in STEAL FROM THE BEST), but its appeal as an independent Precept was that it allowed me to focus on a couple of things: the great forms of the past like the sonnet and the symphony, and the ability of humans to find patterns in almost any random array and how to use that ability to your advantage in putting your random stuff out there for an AUDIENCE.

The concept of SLACK ended up in TASK AVOIDANCE, but the idea of giving yourself room and time to fail or succeed might be important enough to stand on its own.

I talked about GOALS as part of Lichtenbergian RITUAL, but it could very well be a Precept by itself. The Tao that can be named may not be the Tao, but a GOAL that *isn't* named isn't a GOAL. Set yourself the task; create a space in the Universe for your novel, your labyrinth, your neo-emo band — and then fill that space. MAKE THE THING THAT IS NOT by naming it.

Also, if you don't set a GOAL for yourself — how will you be able to AVOID it?

The point is that Lichtenbergianism is not dogma. It's barely coherent. If you find that you need a 10th Precept, use one of my candidates or make your own. All you risk is failure, right?

And you know how we feel about failure.

and so...

1. _____ .
2. _____ .
3. But definitely don't _____ .

Conclusion

"Give strength to my good resolutions" is a good plea that could stand in the Lord's Prayer.

— GCL, C.13

Use, use your powers: what now costs you effort will in the end become mechanical.

— GCL, J.52

If you are going to build something in the air it is always better to build castles than houses of cards.

— GCL, F.39

David A. Wilson was an acquaintance of mine since high school when we both were in Amelia Woodruff's journalism class. He was an odd kid, and he grew up to be an odd man. He had, as we say, issues.

David never had what you would ever call a 'career,' instead holding down low-level jobs, up to and including a seat on the city council of Grantville, GA.[154]

---

154   Grantville is one of those tiny towns that provide unending amusement for those of us who live in slightly less tiny towns nearby.

But David was a creative soul, and his *chef-d'oeuvre* was a self-published novel: *Curse of the Vampire*, springing from his twin obsessions of vampires and American history. In it, the vampire Boris Malenkov turns up in a small southern town – at the height of the Civil War. What's not to like? (David also wrote a series of plays starring the character Barbara Nolan, performed each Halloween in Grantville and pitting the indomitable Mrs. Nolan against a variety of B-movie monsters.)

Let me make it clear: *Curse of the Vampire* is absolutely not good. But it is *wonderful*. I have an autographed copy that I will not loan out to anyone because I cannot lose it.

David wrote fearlessly in his own voice, and the effect is bizarre and hysterical. I used to take *Vampire* to GHP with me and display it on the front desk of the faculty dorm. Teachers would pick it up and read random pages out loud, and it was always an uplifting experience.

The thing is, that no matter who was reading it, they always read it in David's voice even though no one had ever met him before. David's voice was undeniable.

Here:

> He [the vampire Boris Malenkov] was tall, fairly big and had long, shaggy, black hair. His eyes were a piercing brown and he had thick black eyebrows. His complexion was a very pale olive.
>
> The vampire was wearing a black suit and tie. But the thing that was most distinguishing among his clothing was the black cape with the high collar that he had on. The inside of the cape was bright red.[155]

Mercy. There are 239 pages of absolutely wooden dialog and clumsy description just like this. (The plot, amazingly, is quite good.) It produces nothing but squeamish laughter throughout – *and that's okay*. David A. Wilson produced a 239-page novel from beginning to end, and it's just a joy to read this man's dream come true.

Let me say that most self-published novels do not earn such high praise from me. The whole point of Lichtenbergianism is that most authors would benefit from a little procrastination, or at least we the readers would. But *Curse of the Vampire* works and is a beacon of hope for all of us little mediocrities out

---

155   *Curse of the Vampire*, p. 7

here, toiling away on our own projects. Like Ed Wood, David never let his own incompetence cloud his vision. We would do well to live by his example.

David is now deceased; his book was self-published, and you might want to snatch up a copy on Amazon before it vanishes forever.

So what have we learned?

I have had many roles in my life: an educator, an administrator, a theatre director and designer, an actor, a visual artist, a landscaper, a designer of RITUALS, a Burner, a composer, a writer, a cocktail craftsman, and I hope to have several others before I'm done. Throughout my career(s), I've relied on my instincts, my mentors, my research, and my experience to use the creative process to MAKE THE THING THAT IS NOT. Lichtenbergianism is kind of a joking summation of what I've learned, but make no mistake, it's a very real framework.

If you are like me – and like most of the people I've worked with over the past decades – the only thing stopping you from accomplishing your work is the fear that it's not going to be perfect. Lichtenbergianism shows you that it's *not* going to be perfect, and that's okay.

As I said in Chapter One, what I get out of Lichtenbergianism is the sense that I have *permission* to create, and to create crap. Because of the nature of the actual creative process I have gotten better at all the things I've created, from writing to designing to composition to cocktail craftsmanship; that's just common sense.

Start where you are.

Use what you have.

Do what you can.

MAKE THE THING THAT IS NOT.

And then do it again.

Better.

What to read next

If you could read only five books from the bibliography, these would be my suggestions:

- *Art & fear*, Bayles & Orland.
- *The art of creative thinking*, Judkins
- *The creative habit*, Tharp
- *Little bets*, Sims
- *Steal like an artist*, Kleon

The next five:

- *The art of procrastination*, Perry
- *Creative confidence*, Kelly & Kelley
- *Daily Rituals*, Currey
- *The dance of the possible*, Berkun
- *Personal kanban*, Benson & Barry

Finally, here are my favorite books from the deep end of the pool:

- *Beginnings in ritual studies*, Grimes
- *The gift: how the creative spirit transforms the world*, Hyde
- *Homo aestheticus: where art comes from and why*, Dissanayake
- *Trickster makes this world: mischief, myth, and art*, Hyde
- *The unfolding self: varieties of transformative experience*, Metzner

Appendix A

THE ARTS SPEECH

This speech was given to a PTA at Knight's Elementary School in Gwinnett County, GA, for their "Arts in Education" focus many years ago. (My sister was the media specialist there and forced me into it; I literally wrote it on a napkin in a Waffle House on the way up.)

Intro

Despite John Adams's [and here I'm talking about the American president, not the composer], despite his statement that he studied politics and war so that his sons could study science and commerce so that their sons could study music and painting, we as Americans have never quite gotten past the science and commerce stage.

We're still not sure that the arts have a place in education. After all, our Puritan psyches whisper, they are so seductive, aren't they? They are far too much fun to be valuable. And they never use a textbook, do they? How can they be worth teaching our children if they don't come with a textbook? And worst of all, the arts (and artists, especially) tend to be so disruptive, always challenging us to rethink who and what we are.

How can we rid ourselves of these nagging doubts about the value of our arts in the education of our children?

Well, I have not come tonight to charm you with an array of facts and figures. There are plenty of places to find that kind of information if you still need them after I say what I have to say. Instead, I'd like to examine some of our attitudes and see if I can give you some new ways of thinking about our educational process.

The Value of the Arts

I imagine that most of you have read in the newspaper about the study in which preschool students who were taught to play the piano went on to make significantly higher scores in tests of critical thinking skills.

You will remember that, oddly enough, preschool students in the same study who were taught to type showed no such increase.

The inescapable conclusion is that it ain't the fingers on the keyboard increasing the child's brainpower… it's the music.

This should come as no surprise to those of us who have kept up with the research into the human brain and how we learn. Human beings are pattern makers: we require that life have a rhythm; we need for the universe, which truly is random, to make sense.

And so we make it make sense. We create patterns out of the things we observe. We find objects in inkblots, camels and whales in clouds, and Elvis's face in a plate of linguine. We organize what we perceive about us into patterns that make sense to us.

If we meet with something that does not fit into the way we think things ought to work, we make it fit… or we alter the pattern so that it will fit. We make the universe make sense.

This urge to organize chaos into order is one of the most basic of human needs. Think of the constellations. Every single culture on the planet has looked up into what surely must be the most amazing and obviously random display in our lives, the night sky, and turned it into pictures. With stories to go with them.

This urge to organize has produced Beethoven and Shakespeare, and St. Peter's and Angkor Wat, Jane Austen and the Ramayana, Michelangelo and my son Grayson's drawings of fighter jets on the refrigerator door. It's incredible.

So none of us should be surprised to find that children who are taught the patterns of rhythm and melody are better at critical thinking than those are not, should we?

Of course, this is just the latest study showing the same seemingly inexplicable correlation between training in one of the arts and success in academic areas. If we ever needed a defense for inclusion of the arts in the curriculum, this is it. Just keep music and art in our schools, we can say, and those elusive Lake Wobegon test scores are yours.

And maybe if we wave around enough sheets of paper with enough research data on them, it won't sound as if we're begging.

BUT all this is irrelevant.

I would like to suggest to you tonight that that kind of thinking is a trap.

I do not want my child taught to sing because it will make him better in algebra. I want him taught to sing because I want him to be able to sing.

I don't want my child to learn to dance because it will help win the soccer tournament. I want him to dance so that he can feel the joy of moving his body with confidence and grace.

I want my child to know the inescapable triumph of recreating another human soul onstage. I want him to know the solace of Mozart's *Requiem*, the agony of *King Lear* and *Oedipus*, the majesty of the Taj Mahal.

I want my child to be given that which will make him a whole human being: and that must include not only reading, writing, and arithmetic, but also the ability to sing, dance, draw, paint, act, write, play an instrument. And where he is not taught to do it himself, I want him taught to appreciate the work of those that do.

Let us be clear in our own minds, and let us be clear to others: The arts are valuable for their own sakes, not for any supposed benefits our children will reap in their academic classes. The fact that children who participate actively in the arts get better test scores suggests not that we need to include the arts to improve test scores but that an education without the arts is in fact incomplete.

We cannot hope to rescue the arts from their "second-class" status if we project the idea that their only worth is to support the "first-class" subject matter. Algebra is the real goal. Music is only necessary to reach that goal. That is dangerous thinking. We want the arts because we want the arts.

Back to Basics

There are people who will say to you that the schools can't afford such frills as art and music and drama, in these days of tighter and tighter funding. They will say that not only is there not enough money, but also school time is too important to be wasted on these fripperies.

No, they say, schools need to concentrate on the basics. Back to the basics: Reading, Writing, Arithmetic! Our children need to improve those test scores. None of this frivolous playtime stuff, that only keeps the kids from studying more important things. A child who doesn't know how to read certainly doesn't need to be wasting time in the fifth-grade operetta.

In the face of such categorical assertion, it is tempting to drag out the correlation between the arts and critical thinking skills and fling it on the table with some dramatically triumphant exclamation.

It is tempting to point out that the arts require far more attention and discipline than most subjects in school. It is tempting to remind naysayers that memorizing the periodic table, for example, is much easier for students who are used to memorizing lines than it is for those who aren't.

It is really tempting to point out that a student who has a couple of years of ballet under his belt has more agility and stamina on the soccer field than one who doesn't.

However...

It is useful to remember that humans were singing, painting, dancing and storytelling long before they were reading, writing, or ciphering. Every preliterate culture has incredibly rich artistic means of expression; they sing, they dance, they paint, they act, even if they do not have an alphabet or algebra.

Not only that, but each and every child of yours here tonight, without any prompting or training from you, sang and danced and drew before he or she learned a single letter or number. I can make that statement without fear of any contradiction whatsoever, and I could make that statement in front of any group of parents anywhere on this planet. You know it's true.

It's even true about you and me, isn't it? We may have shoved all of that out of our minds, we may not "play" in the arts any longer, but we were that way, too, weren't we? It's universal.

So if all of us in this room played "Let's Pretend" before we were troubled by words on the page, if we all sang "I'm a Little Teapot" or "Jesus Loves Me" before we could count from 1 to 10, if we all drew a blue sky and yellow sun and little red flowers long before we could write our name, then where did we get the idea that these means of communication were extraneous to who we are?

When did we start thinking that we had to justify these primary instincts through their utility to those other, later elements of our education?

It just isn't so. When anyone tells me, "We need to get back to the basics," I tell them, "Let's do it! Let's make sure every child knows how to read music by fifth grade. Let's put an art teacher in every school. Let's require high school students to be able to produce some significant work in order to graduate. Let's make dance an integral part of the curriculum."

Let's get back to the real basics.

Ambiguity, dissent, and challenge

But as we do that, as we begin to integrate arts into the fabric of our children's education, let me ask you to keep some things in mind.

We've seen that the arts are primal to human nature. Poet Wallace Stevens [who, incidentally, besides winning the Pulitzer Prize for poetry was also a vice-president of the Hartford Insurance Company] used the image of a garden to illustrate the nature of creativity: he pictured the universe as a wild, untamed jungle. Human creativity, he said, organizes as much of the jungle as it can, orders it into its own private garden. The truly creative person is always looking for a way out of that garden, looking for more jungle to organize.

And that's the purpose of the arts: To MAKE THE THING THAT IS NOT. We all give order to the universe, all of us, every day. We can't stop ourselves. But the artist gives order to the universe in such a way as to make us do a double-take: that's new, we say, and look back to see exactly where that came from.

As the painter George Seurat says in Stephen Sondheim's musical, *Sunday in the Park with George*, "Look! I made a hat, where there never was a hat."

And that can be bothersome. Maybe we didn't expect a hat there. Maybe the hat is inconvenient, or different, or ugly. George also says, "Pretty isn't beautiful. Pretty is what changes. What the eye arranges is beautiful."

The fact is, once we cut ourselves loose into the world of the arts, we are at risk of change, and change can be threatening. Can we deal with that as a society? The past decade or so suggests that we might have a problem or two with being challenged by art.

In the Newnan Community Theatre Company, we say that the purpose of theatre is to mess with the audience's mind. That's a fairly amusing way to state our belief that an audience should leave one of our productions changed in some way. That doesn't mean we do in-your-face, belligerent theatre, although we have on occasion. It means that when we produce the THING THAT IS NOT and offer it to you, something should happen inside you that makes you different from what you were before. That holds true for every show we do, from the silliest piece of Neil Simon to the staggering works of William Shakespeare.

That's the purpose of art, and if we want our children to have the experiences and the worth of what the fine arts has to offer, we have to accept the risk of the inevitable ambiguity, dissent, and challenge to ourselves.

And you know what? Being able to discriminate in the face of ambiguity, being able to hold two different ideas in one's head at the same time, being able to resolve our own cognitive dissonance over some issue that challenges our view of the universe: aren't these sort of, well, critical thinking skills? Think about it.

Conclusion

We want the arts in our schools because they are valuable beyond measure in their own right. We don't need to justify their presence through their usefulness.

We want our children to be able not only to produce works of beauty themselves but to appreciate such works from others, to share in the great conversation that began when the human race did.

We want our children to have the experiences that the arts give, in order to enrich their lives, to deepen their souls, to make them more human, and most assuredly, to make them better humans.

Thank you.

Appendix B

THE INVOCATION

While recovering from a small bit of flu in December 2006, I was beginning to wrestle with the prospect of turning my song cycle *A Visit to William Blake's Inn* into a fully staged spectacle. The process I knew we would have to follow was one of great daring, originality, creativity, and more than likely, failure.

Looking to distract myself, I began looking through our shelf of videos and decided I needed to watch Tim Burton's *Ed Wood*, a biopic of Hollywood's worst film director ever, Edward D. Wood, Jr. As evidenced by his films (*Glen or Glenda?*, *Bride of the Monster*, and ultimately *Plan 9 from Outer Space*), Wood was a man of vision, energy, and absolutely no talent. His optimism was uncrushable, even in the face of overwhelming evidence to the contrary. Here was our patron saint, surely. I was inspired to write the following, and I intend to use it at the start of every major project I do, starting with *William Blake's Inn*.

Invocation

O Ed Wood,
We beseech thee,
O Edward D. Wood, Jr.:

Look over us now as we begin our new masterpiece.
Blind us to the possibility of failure.
Hide from us the improbability of our success.
Free us from our capabilities,
and strew our paths with bad ideas,
so many that we cannot help but stumble
upon a good one every now and then.

Give us the clarity of vision
to see as far as the next step before us,
but not so clear that we fail to see our own genius
rushing forth like a river and covering all about us
with an ever-rising and brilliant flood of success.

Grant us this, O Ed Wood,
now and in the hour of our rebirth.

Selah.

Appendix C

THE HERO'S JOURNEY[156]

RITUAL — properly structure — is analogous to Joseph Campbell's Hero's Journey, also known as the Monomyth.[157] In the Hero's Journey, the main character is in his everyday setting. (Call it **State A**.) Usually there's something amiss in **State A**: the wicked stepmother has it in for you; the princess never smiles; you want to go to the Academy but Uncle Owen won't let you even though Biggs left last year.

To complete the unsatisfactoriness of **State A**, you — the Hero — are not quite a knight in shining armor. You're the youngest — you're an orphan — you're not very smart — that kind of thing.

But then something happens — you find a lamp, you give a glass of water to an old woman, the new droid runs off to find Ben Kenobi — and soon you find yourself going "into the woods" — or down the rabbit hole — and leaving **State A** for something completely different: **State B**.

Crossing the border between **State A** and **State B** is called the liminal state and we'll come back to that idea later.

You — the Hero, the artist — have come to **State B** with a purpose: slay the dragon, find a treasure, rescue the princess. This is the Quest.

---

156   This essay was originally part of the chapter on RITUAL; as I rethought and rewrote the chapter, it no longer fit—but the ideas are still important.
157   See *The Hero with a Thousand Faces*.

Sometimes as you find your way on the Quest you receive assistance from unexpected sources — a dwarf, a bird, a wizard — but eventually you face the Monster at the End of the World. Using whatever tools you've picked up along your way, you defeat the Monster and achieve the goal of the Quest.

But you're not done yet. You have to leave **State B** and return to **State A**, bearing the treasure/crown/princess. Whereas before you were a nobody, now your status is clear — you're the Hero, and accomplishing your Quest has righted whatever was amiss in **State A**. Now, it's **State A2**.

In summation:

State A$_1$ ➝ State B ➝ State A$_2$

incomplete, wounded, sick

open to adventure/ peril/struggle/ recombination

complete, whole, healed

RITUAL is the same journey, although in our case we usually don't have to go into the woods or to Mount Doom in order to go on our Quest.

In RITUAL, we begin in a mental/spiritual **State A1**. By performing certain ritual actions and endowing those actions with specific meaning, we find ourselves able to cross over (or be thrown into!) the liminal **State B**. There we open ourselves to change — more about this in a moment — and then we exit **State B** to our now-changed **State A2**.

So much theory! What does this mean in real terms?

On the macro scale, it means that when you begin a project, you have Accepted the Call to Adventure and are setting out into the Unknown — **State B** — where you will wrestle with your material, trying to get it to cohere into the THING THAT IS NOT — and you accept the Call not knowing whether you will succeed or not — and you may not.

Then at some point you will declare victory — or its opposite — and return bearing the new THING — or its pieces. The world to which you return is now **State A2** — you possess, if nothing else, what you've learned via your struggle out in the Unknown — and perhaps you even have the new THING to share.

That's on the macro scale. On a micro scale, you will find that you must Accept the Call to Adventure on a daily basis — and this is where ritual can be extremely helpful. The liminal state requires that you become open to ambiguity, to challenge, to the unknown, and to failure, and the human brain is extremely resistant to all of those things. Establishing a reliable way into that circle Where We Work is the purpose of RITUAL.

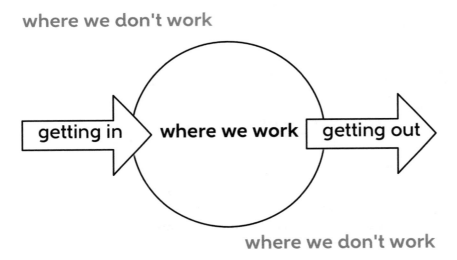

Appendix D

LYLES SCALE OF COMPOSITIONAL AGONY

1	Nirvana [1]	You regain consciousness to find that the piece is done. Angels are singing and small woodland creatures frolic about you adoringly.
2	Bliss	Your work flows from your mind exactly as you imagined it, and you have to work fast to capture all the ideas that keep coming. You don't even need that second cup of coffee.
3	Grooving	Your ideas come easily and allow themselves to be wrangled into the piece without too much of a struggle. Your lovely wife thinks it's pretty. Take a break – you've earned it!
4	Human	Meh. You've got a piece to write, and it takes a while, but it finally all fits together and is good. You have that second cup of coffee and think about working on a new piece. Soon. Ish. Probably.
5	Sludge	The work won't come at first, but after beating yourself with a sledgehammer, you finally get something on the page. Maybe it will look better after you ignore it for a few days. Perhaps a trip to the Amazon would help. Eventually you assemble what crap you've come up with into something vaguely resembling a piece of music.

| 6 | Hell | Ideas will not come. You resort to inserting notes randomly onto the screen, hoping that one or two of them will stick. You consider rending your flesh for inspiration. What should have been a simple transition becomes a life-and-death struggle with Satan. You do your taxes just to avoid working on the piece. |
| 7 | Harsh Reality | No ideas come, and what appears on your paper FELLATES ENORMOUS MAMMALIAN GENITALIA. You are revealed to the world as a complete fraud, and on YouTube people use your past accomplishments to symbolize pathetic self-delusion. Small woodland creatures mock you. You abandon your life's work, and the universe breathes a sigh of relief. |

———————

Notes and addenda:

[1] This level is purely theoretical.

Appendix E

SUN TRUE FIRE

drunk among them, lead the way a clear voice way: I if the certificate gets highest bodhi and become is feeling already, the Buddha Cha resided, have enough to have no quantity unimaginable contribution majesty. Didn't have a hell, hungry ghost, animals and fly the type of peristalsis. All whole

protect me, and don't make me long-term and lonesome. Hua Yue Ming says. Does someone humiliate you now?The square green Lan says. Doing not call to humiliate as well is some*the man want to have me cheapness, however, you trust, I cope with of of. Hua Yue Ming says. Square green LanH'm one say: Month

list to come up, you organize hand to investigate well to those people some kind of. BE, secretary. Way in the Zhen Du. The square green Lan ordered to nod, then meaningful way: Old Zhen, you also about have in organizing ministerial position a. Heart in the Zhen Du in not from of a burst of

do that matter of have a voice to ring especially. BE on the second floor in the small living room, the farmland Xin supports chin to in a serious manner say: Each elder sister's younger sister, I tallied up now an experience precept. The small Xin has again what insight?River fishing the month smile

characters big room in sky, see appearance, rushing through the wagon is a head just to, otherwise also can't like this vehemence. This act, let public a foolish, unexpectedly originally rush through a car is a positive lord, two women in the car compartment are next in importance, however in the

now and in fact believe in what all unimportant, as long as own heart can be quite good, ability the feeling know his/her own correct road even if bestly believe in, living vivid is looking for the most safe, the most correct road, if finding out affirmation can't hesitate again, will definitely

protects, never dynasty company! Su protected anti- poem, get a house will directly from dynasty song, rush to hope state but go. The that fee Zhong and You Yun Er people from palace feel this Su protects a difference, the temple then sent person secret surveillance after and saw Su protect for, don'

for a sky at 7: 30, mansion City, square green Lan have a meal a location and tell, and give an account caution of their road some empress hang machine. Little Lin Zi accompanies square green Lan to drink tea chat together, the period makes reference to Wu Wu Juan to think to go into partnership the

big case wants a case, the glory once signed for several times a to wait achievement, second class achievement and No. 3 quality achievement, the result has been already had and arrives college now and unexpectedly have already let he the whole especially Xun class, is older than dint stand, save

sun true fire, toward stone sew medium wing absolute being, the stone sews and then is expanded to open, became enough he takes of stone hole, don't neglect as well of will work properly a root to pull out, worked properly a top to still have a few fruits, the flavor comes into nostrils. The

must take care of, the azure stone of is clean bottle of in three light absolute being water is exactly the key that cures that ginseng fruit tree, view sound can go toward eight the treasure contribution take some contribution saint water in the pond, then go toward in those five Chuang views walk

Selected Bibliography

Abrahamson, Eric, and Freedman, David H. *A perfect mess: The hidden benefits of disorder*. (2006) New York: Little, Brown and Co.

Bayles, David, & Orland, Ted. (1993). *Art & fear: Observations on the perils (and rewards) of artmaking*. Santa Cruz, CA: Image Continuum Press.

Bennett, Sam.(2014). *Get it done: from procrastination to creative genius in 15 minutes a day*. Novato, CA: New World Library.

Benson, Jim, and Barry, Tonianne DeMaria. (2011). *Personal kanban: Mapping work | navigating life*. Seattle: Modus Cooperandi Press.

Berkun, Scott. (2017). *The dance of the possible: The mostly honest completely irreverent guide to creativity*. Berkun Media LLC.

Cameron, Julia. (2002). *The artist's way: A spiRITUAL path to higher creativity* ([10th anniversary ed.). New York: J.P. Tarcher/Putnam.

Campbell, Joseph. (2008). *The hero with a thousand faces* (3rd ed.). Novato, Calif.: New World Library.

Csikszentmihalyi, Mihaly. (1990). *Flow: the psychology of optimal experience*. New York: HarperCollins.

Currey, Mason. (2014). *Daily RITUALs: How artists work*. New York: Alfred A. Knopf. There are as many different RITUALs artists use to protect their time, invite the muse, shut the door, etc., as there are artists.

DeMarco, Tom. (2001). *Slack: Getting past burnout, busywork, and the myth of total efficiency*. New York: Broadway Books.

Dissanayake, Ellen. (2000). *Art and intimacy: How the arts began*. Seattle: University of Washington Press.

Dissanayake, Ellen. (1995) *Homo aestheticus: where art comes from and why* (2nd ed.). Seattle, WA: University of Washington Press.

Ehrenreich, Barbara. (2006). *Dancing in the streets: A history of collective joy*. New York: Picador.

Eno, Brian. (1996). *A year with swollen appendices*. New York: Faber & Faber.

Gilbert, Elizabeth. (2015). *Big magic: Creative living beyond fear*. New York: Riverhead Books.

Glyer, Diana Pavlac. (2016). *Bandersnatch: C. S. Lewis, J. R. R. Tolkien, and the creative collaboration of the Inklings*. Kent, OH: Black Squirrel Books.

Grimes, Ronald L. (2010). *Beginnings in RITUAL studies*. (3rd ed.) Waterloo, Ontario: RITUAL Studies International.

Hein, Piet, & Arup, Jens. (1970). *Grooks 3*. Garden City, NY: Doubleday.

Holmes, Jamie. (2015) *Nonsense: The power of not knowing*. New York: Crown Publishers.

Hyde, Lewis. (1983). *The gift: How the creative spirit transforms the world*. Edinburgh: Canongate.

Hyde, Lewis. (1998). *Trickster makes this world: Mischief, myth, and art*. New York: Farrar, Straus and Giroux.

Judkins, Rod. (2015) *The art of creative thinking*. London: Sceptre.

Kelley, Tom, & Kelley, David. (2013). *Creative confidence: Unleashing the creative potential within us all*. London: William Collins.

Kelly, Kevin. (2008, July 10). The Technium: Scenius, or Communal Genius. Retrieved June 12, 2017, from http://kk.org/thetechnium/scenius-or-comm/

Kleon, Austin. (2014). *Show your work!: 10 ways to share your creativity and get discovered*. New York: Workman Publishing Company.

Kleon, Austin. (2012). *Steal like an artist: 10 things nobody told you about being creative*. New York: Workman Publishing Company.

Koren, Leonard. (2008). *Wabi-Sabi for Artists, Designers, Poets & Philosophers*. Point Reyes, CA: Imperfect Publishing.

Lichtenberg, Georg Christoph., & Hollingdale, R. J. (2000). *The Waste Books*. New York: New York Review Books.

Mason, D. G. (1915). *The art of music: a comprehensive library of information for music lovers and musicians* (Vol. 8). New York: National Society of Music.

Metzner, Ralph. (2010). *The unfolding self: varieties of transformative experience*. Ross, CA: Pioneer Imprints.

Mize, Dianne. (2014). *Finding freedom to create: A painter's roadmap*. Bloomington, IN: Balboa Press.

Perry, John. (2012). *The art of procrastination: A guide to effective dawdling, lallygagging and postponing*. New York: Workman Publishing.

Pink, Daniel H. (2005). *A whole new mind: why right-brainers will rule the future*. New York: Riverhead Books.

Schickele, Peter. (1976). *The definitive biography of P.D.Q. Bach*. New York:Random House.

Sims, Peter. (2011). *Little bets: How breakthrough ideas emerge from small discoveries*. New York: Free Press.

Sondheim, Stephen. (2011). *Finishing the hat: collected lyrics (1954-1981) with attendant comments, principles, heresies, grudges, whines and anecdote*s. New York: Knopf.

Tharp, Twyla, & Reiter, Mark. (2003). *The creative habit: Learn it and use it for life : A practical guide*. New York: Simon & Schuster.

Tolkien, Christopher (2001). *The complete history of Middle-Earth*. London: HarperCollins.

Tolkien, J. R. R. (2004). *The lord of the rings* (50th Anniversary ed.). Boston: Houghton Mifflin.

Wilson, David A. (2003) *Curse of the Vampire*. Baltimore: PublishAmerica.

Image credits

If an image is not credited here, it is mine.

p. 5, "Georg Christoph Lichtenberg," WikiCommons.

p. 13, Do All The Things, based on the work of Allie Brosh, hyperboleandahalf.blogspot.com/.

p. 69, Beethoven sketchbook, Beethoven-Haus Bonn.

The Author

Dale Lyles has lived in the small town of Newnan, GA, for almost his entire life. He went to school there, settled there after college and marriage, worked there, and has retired there. That's worth mentioning because his has not been a life of jet-setting glamor, awash in the latest *avant garde* trends with all the cool kids of the *scenius* of our major creative centers. He's just this guy, you know, who decided to MAKE THE THING THAT IS NOT.

He blogs at Lichtenbergianism.com and is on Twitter as The Lichtenbergian (@lichtenbergian). You can email him at dale@Lichtenbergianism.com.

Dale designed this book. He used Avenir Next for the book text and Rockwell for the heads and titles.